Finding JESUS on UPSIDE DOWN DAYS

Jill A. Miller

illustrated by Brad Woodard

FAMILY DEVOTIONS FROM THE BARNYARD

New Growth Press, Greensboro, NC 27401

Cover/Interior Design: Brad Woodard with the assistance of Ryan Peters

ISBN: 978-1-64507-261-4 (Print)
ISBN: 978-1-64507-262-1 (eBook)

Library of Congress Cataloging-in-Publication Data on file
Names: Miller, Jill, A., author. | Woodard, Brad, illustrator.
Title: Finding Jesus on upside down days : family devotions from the barnyard / Jill A. Miller.
Description: Greensboro, NC : New Growth Press, [2022] | Includes bibliographical references and index. | Summary: "As Jill takes care of her animals, enjoying what the Creator has made, God takes her upside-down soul and sets it right-side up"-- Provided by publisher.
Identifiers: LCCN 2022011416 (print) | LCCN 2022011417 (ebook) | ISBN 9781645072614 | ISBN 9781645072621 (ebook)
Subjects: LCSH: Animals--Prayers and devotions. | Animals--Religious aspects--Christianity. | Families--Religious life.
Classification: LCC BV4596.A54 M55 2022 (print) | LCC BV4596.A54 (ebook) | DDC 231.7--dc23/eng/20220321
LC record available at https://lccn.loc.gov/2022011416
LC ebook record available at https://lccn.loc.gov/2022011417

Printed in Canada

29 28 27 26 25 24 23 22   1 2 3 4 5

To Andrew
My barnyard companion,
who always made sure the
buckets were filled before
he ran up the driveway
to catch the school bus.

CONTENTS

WELCOME!

PLEASE COME INTO MY BARNYARD AND MEET MY ANIMALS. I like to call them my friends. I love it when my daughter Kim, my grandkids, and neighborhood kids come to visit—and I'm not the only one! My friends love it when children come because they know I'll break out the animal crackers. The sound of the red lid turning on the plastic bear cookie jar makes the barnyard sing.

Chuckie and Kisses bray excitedly. They have been together since they were three weeks old. They were born in New York. My husband Paul gave them to me for my birthday. One day after teaching kindergarten, I found carrots and a balloon tied to my mailbox. Driving down the driveway, standing in the field, were two mini–Jerusalem donkeys! As soon as I saw their ears, bellies, and deep-set brown eyes, it was love at first sight—for all three of us.

You see, over the years, Paul got sad watching me be sad when my dogs and goats died. So Paul got me "the boys," Chuckie and Kisses. They could live to be forty years old! Maybe one of my grandkids will take care of them after I go to heaven.

Oh boy! What is that banging? It's Chezlee, and he desperately wants his breakfast. Goodness, he rams his horns into the door just to tell me he's hungry. All 180 pounds of him. You would think he's starving, but after you look at him, you'll know he's well fed! Edith, Chezlee's sister, yells a lot. She is always trying to keep him in line. And that can be a challenge. Chezlee and Edith are called fainting goats. They faint when they are happy or scared. And I mean *faint*. Backs on the ground and four hooves stiff in the air!

Then there is Nuah. That is the Hebrew word for "rest." Paul likes the Hebrew language. He once tried learning it but never got beyond naming my animals. Nuah is nervous, and she rarely rests because she's so stressed. But Nuah goes nuts over treats! She is a sweet, small pygmy goat who loves to climb and jump.

We don't live on a farm, but we live next to a beautiful farm owned by Mr. Beer. He is a real farmer, and he loves Jesus. Mr. Beer tells me I'm a wannabe farmer. It's true! But I want to wait to be a real farmer until I'm in heaven—where there won't be bugs or disease or bad weather or animals that die. But I'd still love to drive a tractor, even now. I'm just not sure Mr. Beer is up to giving me lessons!

When I share my final animal crackers with my friends, and I close the gate behind me, I almost hear them say, "Thank you, Grammy."

Here come my sweet dogs, Anaiah and Tully, greeting me with wagging tails and a few happy barks. Anaiah is the angel dog. She's even white like an angel. She would love just to sit with kids under a big tree. Tully, on the other hand, prefers chasing tennis balls until your arm feels like it's going to fall off.

Many days seem to be upside down. Topsy-turvy. Right from the get-go, the day seems out of control. But in the craziness, there can be peace. Psalm 37:23 says, "The Lord directs the steps of the godly. He delights in every detail of their lives" (NLT).

When I go out to the barnyard every day, God pops those "details" into my head. As I take care of the animals and see all he has made, he takes my upside-down soul and sets it right-side up. I hope these stories do the same for you!

I'm so glad you're meeting my friends. I hope you enjoy them as much as I do!

God is so good,

Jill for all

CAST OF CHARACTERS

Paul is my husband. We've been married for fifty years!

Kim is the fourth of our six children. She has several disabilities, one of which is autism. Kim uses a computer and sign language to talk. Each day, she walks several different dogs while their "mommies and daddies" work. This is her job.

Mr. Beer is our next-door neighbor. He owns a beautiful farm that grows wheat, corn, and soy. He also has about fifty cows.

Chuckie and **Kisses** are miniature Jerusalem donkeys. They have been together since they were three weeks old. We adopted them at age three years. Now they are about thirteen and could live till they are forty years old! I call them "the boys."

Chezlee and **Edith** are twins. They are fainting goats. And they really faint!

Berachah is an introverted pygmy goat.

Getty is a pygmy goat, and she had a kid (baby) named Nuah. **Nuah** is always nervous when meeting new friends.

Tove was a beautiful golden retriever. She had seven puppies, one of which is **Hessid**.

Anaiah is a golden retriever. She's actually white, not golden.

Tully is a golden retriever who enjoys welcoming people into our house. One day he pulled Kim's bedspread off her bed and dragged it down a flight of steps, just to give the plumber a "gift."

Bruiser is a dog who lived down our street. He enjoyed playing with Tove and Hessid.

Cooper is a beagle. He is also an escape artist.

WHY?

We live next to Mr. Beer. He has been a farmer for more than sixty-five years! He has cows, chickens, horses, and sheep. I enjoy talking to Mr. Beer and learning how he grows corn, soy, and wheat. I also like to hear about his animals. Mr. Beer is a busy farmer. That is how he makes his living.

One day, after I had fed my friends, Mr. Beer drove up to me on his tractor. He asked, "Why do you have these animals?"

"I just love animals and enjoy them," I said.

"Do you get milk from the goats to sell?" asked Mr. Beer.

"No, I just love the goats and enjoy watching them play," I said.

"Maybe you could make goat cheese. People enjoy eating that," responded Mr. Beer.

"No, I have the goats to make me laugh. They are funny to watch—how they jump from rock to rock—how they chase one another around. Really, I just enjoy the goats and love them."

"Oh. I never heard of that before. Well, what are you going to do with the boys? Are they going to do tricks? Are they going to pull your grandkids in a cart?" The questions flowed out of Mr. Beer's mind as he suggested ways the animals could make money for me.

"Mr. Beer, I just love to brush the boys and watch them play. They will run around the field as if they are great big dogs playing tug of war with their toys."

Mr. Beer chuckled and replied, "I have never heard of that before!"

"Have you seen Paul and I walk the boys? I love to take them on a quiet Sunday walk down your gravel path. As we walk, they pull out their favorite weeds and chomp away. After our walk, as I take off their lead, Kisses will give me one of his hugs."

"No. I haven't ever seen you walk them, or anybody else walk donkeys! And I have never seen or felt a donkey hug me or anybody else!" replied Mr. Beer. "You mean to tell me that you don't make any money from your animals?"

"Nope. I just love and enjoy them."

One day as I was with the boys, the thought came to me that I don't have to do anything special for God to love me either. God loves and enjoys me, just like I love and enjoy my friends.

DEUTERONOMY 7:6–8a

You are a holy nation. The LORD your God has set you apart for himself. He has chosen you to be his special treasure. He chose you out of all the nations on the face of the earth to be his people. The LORD chose you because he loved you very much. He didn't choose you because you had more people than other nations. In fact, you had the smallest number of all. The LORD chose you because he loved you.

PROVERBS 17:17

A friend loves at all times. They are there to help when trouble comes.

THE BOYS

I have a small barn that looks like a shed. In most sheds, you find lawn mowers and bicycles. But in our small barn, you will find animals. I have two miniature Jerusalem donkeys. They are both boys, and they are brothers. They are about four years old. Their names are Chuckie and Kisses. Chuckie is a good name for a boy donkey, but I don't think Kisses is. Once you get to know Kisses, you will understand why that's his name.

Have you ever come home from school after a hard day? Maybe your friends left you out of a game at recess. Maybe you got a C on a spelling test that you worked hard on and had studied for and had written each word three times. Maybe someone told a story about you, and it wasn't kind or true. How would you feel? Rotten. Sad. Like you wanted to be alone.

Well, sometimes when I go out to the boys, it is after I have had one of those days. Chuckie and Kisses like to be brushed, they like fresh water and hay, and they love animal crackers or their special cookies. Without saying a word, I will start my work. Cleaning, feeding, brushing, and watering. As I stoop down to clean up the hay, Kisses will stand right next to me. All of a sudden, I feel a warm, heavy weight on my back. It is Kisses's head. After he leans his head over my back, he will pull me close to him. I am getting a donkey hug!

Kisses knows when I am sad. He knows when I need a hug. I don't have to tell him how I feel; he just knows. What a good friend!

THE GOATS

1 CORINTHIANS 13: 6–7

Love . . . always protects.

I also have goats in the barnyard. Two of them are twins, and they are three years old. The girl is named Edith. The boy is named Chezlee. Now, Chezlee and Edith are fainting goats. When they get either really happy or really scared, they faint—right over on their backs—with their little hooves in the air.

Chuckie, Kisses, Edith, and Chezlee like to eat together, sleep together, and play together. They are all friends.

One day, when I was unpacking groceries from the car, I heard Edith yell. It wasn't a happy yell. It was more like a scared yell. I dropped the bag of groceries and ran into the pasture to see what was going on. Kisses was standing close to Edith with a worried face. Edith had fainted and was on her back with her hooves straight in the air, petrified. I waited for Edith to get up and begin walking. As she did, Kisses began to relax. I went back to my car and finished putting away the groceries.

A few days later, I saw my friends from my kitchen window. They were playing together and having a fun time. Remember, when fainting goats get happy, what do they do? Faint! Kisses and Edith were enjoying chasing, pushing, and rolling a red ball. The more they chased, the stiffer Edith got. Oh no! One, two, three—down for the count! There goes Edith, hooves in the air. I could tell by looking at Kisses that he was upset. (You know how you can tell what people are thinking by looking at their face? Like when someone is mad at you?) Kisses thought he hurt Edith and that she was on the ground because of him. But Edith was on the ground because she fainted from having so much fun.

So, like a good friend, Kisses tried to get Edith back on her feet—or should I say hooves. The more Kisses tried to help Edith, the stiffer Edith got—and the stiffer Edith got, the more scared Kisses became. Get the picture? So now Kisses really knew it was up to him to help Edith. With determination, Kisses took Edith's back leg and began to pull her toward the barn. You see, the boys are very smart.

Donkeys know that the safest place for an animal to be is inside a barn, not out in the pasture. An animal, like a coyote, looks for animals stranded in pastures, and Kisses knew he had to protect his friend, Edith.

At this point, I ran out and tried to help both of them. I told Kisses that Edith really was okay, and that she would be able to get up and walk in a couple minutes after he let go of her leg. Then I told Edith that she didn't have to be afraid—that Kisses was really trying to protect her.

Good friends protect each other—even the ones that faint!

THE MORNING WALK

PSALM 37:4a

Find your delight in the LORD.

This morning Hessid and I went for a walk. Our house is right next to Mr. Beer's beautiful farm, and he allows us to walk down a path between his pastures. This allows Hessid to be unleashed, and for her and I to waddle down the road at our own pace. Sometimes in the morning, when it is still foggy, we can see the blurry, gray shapes of deer slowly grazing on the fresh green grass—or a fox running back to its den to take care of its precious kits. Hessid and I love to go on these walks!

However, lately Hessid and I have been sad on our morning walks. This is because Tove, Hessid's mom, died recently. It was always Tove, Hessid, and me on the path between the pastures. Tove was never without Hessid, and Hessid was never without Tove. Every morning, they always ended up chasing each other by the end of the walk. I can still see their beautiful, full, golden tails wagging in unison as they ran after each other.

But now it is just Hessid and me.

To add a little "life" to our walk, I bring three dog biscuits with me. Before I leave the house, Hessid waits for the clunk of the doggie jar lid and the sound of me grabbing three bone-shaped veggie biscuits. I put all three biscuits in my sweatshirt pocket, and then Hessid and I leave the house and trot off down the path together. Hessid stays close to me, looking up at me regularly to make sure that I will remember to give her the treats. At the end of the path, where we turn around to come back to the house, I give her the first treat. I break the biscuit into three pieces so Hessid is able to taste the treat and not do the big gulp.

On our way back to the house, Hessid is close to me. With each step, I feel her soft furry side hit my leg. She looks up at me with her beautiful, deep, brown eyes. She has the look of such loyalty and devotion. Or maybe the look of, "Hey! I know you have two more treats in your pocket!" Then I see her front paws lift off the ground, and her nose pokes my sweatshirt pocket. Okay, forget the devotion; this is about food.

I thought to myself, *Am I like Hessid, with Jesus? Do I hang out right next to him because he gives me goodies?*

I want Hessid to love me—not just the treats. Jesus wants me to love him and not just the gifts he gives me!

I want Hessid to know I love her. Jesus wants me to know he loves me.

I want Hessid to stay next to me and enjoy me because of me. Jesus wants me to stay next to him and enjoy him because of him.

ANAIAH

Anaiah is our one-year-old pup. We got her when she was eight weeks old. She's a sweetie, and she has a lot of energy. At twelve weeks old, I took her to a puppy class to learn basic "manners" for dogs. After eight weeks, she received her "Good Canine Citizenship" reward. (Even though she still enjoyed finding and eating my dirty socks.)

As time passed, I noticed how much Anaiah enjoyed people. She liked meeting new people, and they enjoyed meeting her. So I decided to train Anaiah to become a therapy dog. A therapy dog is trained to go to places like hospitals, schools, and nursing homes. There, it finds people who might be sad, scared, or just not feeling well. The dog will sit down right next to a person and allow the person to pet them until they have had their fill of love.

So Anaiah and I jumped into the car and went to our very first class. We were going to learn how to be a *really* good girl. We went to a class where we were the youngest and the smallest, and in "kindergarten" compared to the other dogs who were older and bigger, and in "middle school." Anaiah was nervous. I was nervous.

Anaiah had a hard time listening to me during the classes. Actually she did not listen to me at all. At the end of the class, Anaiah and I walked slowly back to our car and were happy to be on our way to a safe, quiet house.

Anaiah and I went to class for the next two weeks. Anaiah still wasn't listening to me. She wanted to be cool and play with her new big friends. (Kind of like when you're a kid and you don't want to listen to your parents in front of your friends.) The dog trainer told me to get a special collar. It was called a prong collar. When I put it on Anaiah, little prongs pinched her neck. Ouch.

The next class, the prong collar went on. Anaiah stopped playing with her friends and began to listen to every word I said. She obeyed me and did all the things I asked her to do.

On my way home from the dog-training class, with Anaiah sound asleep in the back of my car, I thought about how I wished Anaiah would have just obeyed my kind voice. If she had, I would not have needed to use the collar.

Sometimes I think God talks to me kindly and tells me how to love others—and how to do what is right—and I don't listen either. But God loves me so much that he sometimes brings things into my life that hurt (like Anaiah's collar). Because then, I am able to hear his voice.

Jesus, please help me listen to your voice, so you won't need to use a prong collar in my life to get my attention. Amen.

PSALM 32:9

Don't be like a horse or a mule. They can't understand anything. They have to be controlled by bits and bridles. If they aren't, they won't come to you.

HERE COMES THE STORM!

PSALM 32:7

You are my hiding place. You will keep me safe from trouble. You will surround me with songs sung by those who praise you because you save your people.

This morning I went to the barn. The boys, Chuckie and Kisses, and the goats greeted me with their usual burst of energy—looking and prodding for the carrots and animal crackers that I hide in my sweatshirt. I turned on the radio. (The goats have almost destroyed my radio!) But what was different today was that the radio was warning us of a coming storm—a storm of "historic proportions"—possibly record-breaking snowfalls. I felt stressed. But the gang didn't. They had no idea what was coming.

I started working and cleaned up the barn from the previous night. I gave everybody clean water. I made sure that the two water buckets were plugged in so their water wouldn't freeze.

I distributed fresh hay for everyone—putting extra "flakes" in the racks just in case the storm was as bad as predicted. I knew that some of the extra hay would fall from the racks, providing a warm bed for the gang to rest on.

I brushed the boys and told them about the coming storm, and that I would come and check on them to make sure they and the goats were okay. I don't think they got the whole gist of the conversation.

I looked at the flag to see which direction the wind was coming from. I closed the appropriate barn doors to keep it from coming in, while leaving the other doors open. That way, the gang could get out if they wanted to check the sights and sounds.

I kept the lights on. Sometimes I get tired of the gray, dark winter days too. I left the barn, with everybody eating and content.

I do not know when storms (really hard things) will come into my life, but Jesus said they *will*. Jesus is a perfect preparer. (Way better than me.) He gives me everything I need to get through each storm.

PSALM 121:5

The LORD watches over you.

THE STORM IS HERE

It is dark. The only light I see is from the spotlight that is on the side of the barn. From that small light, I see huge swirls of snow encircling the barn.

It is cold. So cold that the last time I went outside, I had a hard time opening the gate because ice coated the lock.

It is noisy. The howl of the wind keeps me from hearing anything else.

The gang is hunkered down. They have made beds for themselves from the hay that has dropped from their feeding racks. They roll into a ball and stay close to one another to share their warmth.

On my way back to the house, I have made sure all of the gates are shut. The fence is secure. No animals can come into our pasture and into the barn. (We have coyotes near our house.)

To my friends, I am sure it looks like I am in the house, asleep like they are. Just another ordinary night. But tonight is different. The storm is here. Once I get into bed, I am restless. Every time I turn (and that is a lot of times!), I look out to the spotlight to see if all looks well.

Long before dawn, I put on my boots and snow jacket, find my warmest gloves, and trudge through the snow to the gang. I want them to know that I am here and have been watching them. Actually, I watch over them even more during a storm. They don't see me watching, but I am.

Jesus is like that. The worse the "storm" we are in, the more he is watching. He is aware of all the dangers surrounding us. He is the best Shepherd.

FOOTPRINTS IN THE SNOW

It's just so cold. Last night's snow is swirling and dancing around me as I am walking across the lawn to the barn. With my head down and tucked against my chest, my eyes follow and look at the ground. After a snow, I enjoy seeing what is usually unseen: *footprints*.

Along the edge of the fence, I spot lots of bunny footprints. I can "see" them hop! Around the goats, I spot bird's footprints. I can "see" them jump! Along the driveway, I spot deer prints. Maybe three or four deer. I can "see" them leap! The paws of the fox go from the thicket and around our swing set. I can "see" them trot! The raccoon enjoys checking out the box of grain in the garage. I can "see" him trying to pry open the box!

All of this went on under the light of the moon, as we were snoring away in our warm beds. Psalm 104:20 says, "You, LORD, bring darkness, and it becomes night. Then all the animals of the forest prowl around." There is a lot of prowling around our house! I love it.

As I open the gate to the field, I see the boys in their shed, trying to protect themselves from the wind. (They do not like wind!) Their eyes are covered by their long bangs, and their winter coat is thick and shaggy. They munch on the sweet carrots that I hold for them. The goats scamper about, greeting me with their sweet noises, anticipating a yummy breakfast. After everyone has eaten, I walk around the fence, checking to make sure it is secure.

I see footprints. They kind of look like a dog's, but they are not. They are far apart but not running or leaping. They look like a lope, or long stride. We have seen them before. The footprints are from a coyote, and they are dotted along the inside of the fence.

One of the reasons we have the boys is to protect the goats. Some people call donkeys "guardian donkeys." Their job is to protect the goats from animals like coyotes. If a coyote decided to attack the goats, the boys would chase them away.

Do you know that the Bible says that Satan prowls around looking for ways to hurt us? We don't have donkeys that guard us though. Instead, we have great, big angels.

PSALM 91:11

The LORD will command his angels to take good care of you.

OH NO, YOU'RE EATING THE WRONG THING!

MATTHEW 4:4 NLT

But Jesus told him, "No! The Scriptures say, 'People do not live by bread alone, but by every word that comes from the mouth of God.'"

Last night, Paul fed the barnyard residents. The goats usually get grain, hay, and fresh water. The boys only get hay and fresh water. (Sometimes I give them animal crackers.)

Paul likes to save money. That means he can be "sparse" with the hay.

When I came out this morning to clean up the barnyard, there was not one bit of hay left. But there was also something else that was missing. The door. The boys *ate* the door!

It was a cold night. When it is cold, animals eat more because they have to stay warm. They (and we) eat food to give them energy to stay warm.

I can just imagine last night. The boys were chewing up the hay. Pushing it around with their noses. Chew. Chew. All gone.

"What should we eat?" they asked each other. "How about the door!" Chuckie exclaimed.

Chomp. Chomp. Chomp. There goes the barn door. Little slivers on the floor and big slivers into their tummies.

I can be a lot like the boys. To get my energy, I eat the wrong things. I don't mean like cookies and cake and bright yellow cheese curls. Jesus says that I should live and get my energy from his words.

Sometimes I try to get my energy from friends, making people happy, and trying to look "hip." (This is really hard to do when you are a grammy.)

But Jesus says that I should get my energy from his words. His words are the Bible. I need to read and think about what Jesus's words say—and then do them. That is how Jesus wants me to get my energy.

BRUISER

LUKE 15:3–6

Then Jesus told them a story. He said, "Suppose one of you has 100 sheep and loses one of them. Won't he leave the 99 in the open country? Won't he go and look for the one lost sheep until he finds it? When he finds it, he will joyfully put it on his shoulders and go home. Then he will call his friends and neighbors together. He will say, 'Be joyful with me. I have found my lost sheep.'"

Climbing over the piles of snow, with five bowls of goat food and two carrots stuffed in the pocket of my jacket, I came to a stop. The snow under the gate had melted the day before, and now the gate was frozen into a puddle. I set the bowls down and gave the gate one good lift up and shove. Open!

The boys are very glad to see me. They are glad to see anyone. As Kisses put his nose into my pocket, the goats scurry into their positions, waiting for me to set their bowls down with a "Good morning!"

As I was reaching for the rake, I heard barking. A lot of barking. Looking up, I saw Anaiah excited and happy to see her friend and neighbor, Bruiser. I can always tell when Anaiah sees Bruiser at our house. She goes crazy!

Bruiser lives at the end of our street, about one-half mile away. He is a nine-year-old yellow lab. He lives in a house with young kids who like to open the back door. This comes in handy because Bruiser lives to charge out of any opened door!

Once outside, Bruiser is hard to bring back inside. He has his favorite places to visit. He has favorite people to visit. He has favorite dogs to visit. Anaiah is one of those dogs.

Bruiser will play with Anaiah for a while, and after he and Anaiah are all tuckered out, he will wander into our garage. At this point, I will walk to Bruiser, get the phone number off of his dog tag, and call his owners. As soon as I talk to Bruiser's "mommy," she quickly jumps into her car and comes over. As her car comes down our driveway, Bruiser gets lower to the ground and lays like a sphinx. When his mommy opens her car door, Bruisers ears go back with each of her footsteps, toward the back door. "Bruiser, get in!" Bruiser jumps in. As Bruiser is chauffeured down our driveway, he keeps his gaze on Anaiah.

Well, this day was different. It was too cold for Anaiah and Bruiser to play outside for longer than a few minutes. It felt like twenty degrees below zero. So I put down the rake and went over to get his phone number to call his mommy. (You would think I have the phone number memorized, but I don't.) But Bruiser did not have on his collar.

So, I went into the house and got my keys and opened my car door. Bruiser jumped in, and off we went back to his house.

His mommy was so glad to see him and told me that "the girls" had left the door opened as they measured the newly fallen snow—and off he went.

That night, I shared with Paul about Bruiser's visit. "Why do you take him back? He knows his way home!"

I thought about the times Jesus brings me back to himself and his house when I wander off. Sometimes I feel Jesus look at me with compassion and say, "Jill, come with me. I'll make sure you get home."

WILL WINTER EVER END?

When I wake up in the morning, one of the first things I look at is our neighbor's American flag. I look to see if it is drooping or waving. Most of these winter days, it has been wildly waving.

Then I go downstairs and look at the thermometer. It is twenty-four degrees. But it is April! While I am reading my Bible, I start counting how many days it has been cold. More than one hundred days. That is a long time! That is a long winter! Will it ever end?

After breakfast, Paul bundles up in his down coat. He puts on his hat and gets Hessid and Anaiah ready for their morning walk. At the same time, I put on my down jacket and walk out to the garage. In the garage, I put on my "donkey sweatshirt." (It smells just like the boys, no matter how many times I wash it!) Then I put on my boots and walk out to my friends.

Everyone is huddled in the barn. Getty and Nuah look like one goat, they are so close. Berachah is in a tight ball on the top shelf. Edith and Chezlee are on the floor of the barn burrowed under the hay. On the other side of the barn are Kisses and Chuckie. They hate the wind. They are standing against the back wall of the barn, keeping as far from the wind as they can. They are standing like statues.

For the past month, my first sentence to the boys is, "Spring is on its way!" I am beginning to wonder myself if this is true. In winter, it always takes longer to clean out the barn. More poo. More hay. Electric buckets. (These are buckets that stay warm so the water never freezes.) It is a hassle to fill the buckets because the hose often freezes. When I rake out the hay, the boys don't want to move. Try moving a donkey that doesn't want to move. After cleaning the barn, the animals get grain and fresh hay. Everyone has a particular place to eat their grain and a special spot for their hay.

After finishing with my friends, I tell them, "Hang in there!" Trudging back to the garage, I hang up my donkey sweatshirt (I can't put it in the house because it stinks), pull off my boots, and walk back to the house with my chin tucked to my chest, avoiding the wind.

If feels so good in the house. I grab my warm coffee and look out the window. The boys are back in the corner, avoiding the wind. Their bangs almost cover their big brown eyes, and I see their shaggy coat is still.

Our lives have seasons too. When we go through a long, hard time, it is kind of like winter. But winter does end—at just the right time. And so will our hard times.

ISAIAH 49:8a

The LORD says . . . , "When it is time to have mercy on you, I will answer your prayers. When it is time to save you, I will help you. I will keep you safe."

YIKES! I'M NAKED!

LUKE 3:11a

John answered, "Anyone who has extra clothes should share with the one who has none."

Winter is taking its good old time leaving, and what a winter it has been! It feels like forever since the sun has warmed our faces. But now the weather is starting to change. And with that change comes the shedding of the animals' coats. Do you ever wear your winter coat on warm days? I am sure you throw it into the back of your closet once the temperature starts rising.

Well, the barnyard residents can't throw off their coats (plus they don't have a closet to put their coats in), so God has them shed their coats. And that's just what they do. It is a slow shed because, in early spring, it still gets pretty cold at night.

One morning after feeding the goats, I noticed a bald spot on Getty. *Hmm*, I thought to myself. *Maybe one of her barnmates bit off some fur while they were playing (it can get a little rough).*

The next day, I went out and noticed two bald spots on Getty. *Hmm*, I thought to myself. *Interesting*.

On the third day, while I was brushing Getty, lots and lots of fur came out. *Hmm*, I thought to myself. *Well, we did have a hard winter, maybe she just had an extra heavy coat*.

On the fourth day, I peeked out of my kitchen window and spotted Getty. *Hmm*, I thought to myself. *She is pink with brown spots*.

I quickly went out, with some carrots, to find out why Getty was pink with brown spots. *Hmm*, I thought to myself. *She is naked!*

Getty had no fur! And she was shivering!

I hurried back into the house and found Paul's thermal shirt. I cut the sleeves short because Getty has short legs, and then went outside to put it on Getty.

Getty had never worn a shirt before, so she was a little hesitant about putting her head through the neck and her legs through the sleeves, but being the trusting goat that she is, she allowed me to dress her in Paul's now cut-off shirt.

The other goats had never seen a goat wearing a shirt, so they did some serious staring! While I was cleaning up, everyone accepted the new look of Getty—especially Getty herself.

When I came back into the house, I told Paul what happened to Getty and how I solved the problem. He was a little surprised that I cut up his shirt. I explained to him that he had two thermal shirts. (I did not own any thermal shirts, or I would have used mine.) I explained that the Bible says if we have two coats we should give one to someone in need.

SIGNS

Our neighbor's flag is still waving strong. But since it is no longer dark in the morning, I can see it as soon as I wake up. I open the door to let out Hessid and Anaiah, and I hear more than the wind. I hear birds! I hear different songs!

After my cup of coffee, I grab two carrots then walk out to the garage. I wiggle my big feet into my chilly plastic boots and get a strong whiff of the boys as I pull my sweatshirt over my head. As I am laying out the five plastic bowls on the garage floor and fill each with grain, the loud chorus starts. The goats know their tummies will be full in a few minutes.

As I walk to my friends, the air just feels different. It smells different. Can I tell them that I think it's here? Is winter over? Is spring finally springing? Yes!

So as Chuckie and Kisses are enjoying their carrots, I break the news to them. "Spring is here! Very soon you won't need hay because this brown field is going to be bright green. And no more electric bucket. Yeah! You can have your big red tub again."

The boys didn't seem to do anything special to celebrate. No jig. No party. But I knew what was coming for them. Days to lie out in the sun. No more hiding in the barn keeping out of the cold and wind. Lots of fun running around and playing.

The signs of spring. You could easily miss them, so you have to slow down and look and listen. The sun is coming up earlier and going down later, the animals are busy gathering food for their newborn babies, birds are busy finding twigs to build their nests, and those bright colors are beginning to explode!

Jesus tells us a story about the signs of his second coming. Just like a branch pops open with a bud to tell us spring is here, there will be signs to tell us that Jesus is coming soon. And the way that I look forward to spring doesn't even compare with the way I look forward to Jesus coming back!

So start looking for those miraculous signs from heaven, showing us that Jesus's return will be soon.

LUKE 21:29–33 NLT

Then [Jesus] gave them this illustration: "Notice the fig tree, or any other tree. When the leaves come out, you know without being told that summer is near. In the same way, when you see all these things taking place, you can know that the Kingdom of God is near. I tell you the truth, this generation will not pass from the scene until all these things have taken place. Heaven and earth will disappear, but my words will never disappear."

PSALM 32:7

You are my hiding place. You will keep me safe from trouble. You will surround me with songs sung by those who praise you because you save your people.

A HIDING PLACE

I just came in the house from sweeping out our garage. Sometimes it bugs me that we don't have garage doors because during the winter lots of leaves and dirt blow into the garage. So every spring, I get our big broom (the kind custodians use at your school) and give the garage a good sweep. If you happened to drive by our house while I am sweeping, you would see a cloud of dirt swooshing and bellowing from the garage. Not only do we get dirt and leaves in our garage, but sometimes we also get critters, and apparently this winter was no exception.

As the dust settled from the sweeping, I noticed teeny-tiny pieces of blue plastic. I followed the trail, which began at our pool cover and led to the hosing that we use to clean our pool. There was a hole in the hose about the size of a tennis ball! The hole was overflowing with leaves and tiny pieces of our pool cover.

All of a sudden, I had a picture in my mind of some skinny, hungry, cold, shivering mouse in a frenzy trying to get warm. They looked around for a place of protection. Ta-da, our pool hose! The hose filled with plastic and leaves did the trick and kept them out of the cold. Protection. They had protection.

There are times in our lives when we are in a frenzy, just like that mouse. We might not be cold, but we might feel lonely. We might not be hungry, but we might feel worried. We might not be shivering, but we might feel lost. Lots of things can put us in a frenzy.

But just like the mouse made a safe place to hide for protection, we have a safe place to hide too. We can hide in Jesus.

NOW WE GO HOME

PHILIPPIANS 3:20 NLT

But we are citizens of heaven, where the Lord Jesus Christ lives. And we are eagerly waiting for him to return as our Savior.

Every morning I exercise. First, I run two miles, then I walk two miles. Every year I get slower and slower.

One morning after my exercise, I was trying to get work done. Anaiah was jumping all over Hessid. After I told Anaiah to give Hessid a break, she left Hessid then started chewing and licking my toes. It is hard to work when you are being tickled by a puppy. That morning, I made two decisions. The first decision was that Anaiah had more energy than I did. The second was to take Anaiah along with me on my early morning exercise routine.

To allow Anaiah room to run at her pace, I got her a leash that extends out when she goes ahead of me and contracts back when she slows down and runs next to me.

Our morning jaunt starts with us running up and down the farm road that is next to our house. This road goes to Mr. Beer's house. In the summer, the road is lined on both sides with corn. As the corn grows in the hot summer, it gradually shades the road. In the winter, I see the winter wheat that is waiting to pop up in the spring.

We finish running when Mr. Beer's farm road ends. His road ends on our street. Now we stay on our street and walk to the left and pass our driveway. Anaiah pulls hard toward the driveway as if to say, "Hey! Here is our house!" I tell her, "We are going to the mailbox." Anaiah doesn't want to go to the mailbox; she wants to go home. But I am bigger, so I win. As we continue on our street, Anaiah relaxes and enjoys walking. We make it to the mailbox.

Now we turn around, and I tell Anaiah, "We are going to the stop sign." With the leash in my hand, Anaiah proudly prance's next to my left side. But as we come close to our driveway, Anaiah lunges ahead and tries to drag me down the driveway to our house. I tell Anaiah again, "We are going to the stop sign."

Once we have moved from our driveway, Anaiah settles again into a sweet walk. We walk to the end of our street and to the stop sign. Then we turn around again. This time I tell Anaiah, "Now we go home!" For the rest of the walk, she pulls me, anxious to get to our driveway and then home.

When we enter the driveway, I remove Anaiah's leash, and off she goes to find Hessid, who is waiting for her on the porch. (Don't worry; Hessid has a short walk too!)

Anaiah loves to go home.

Jesus tells us that our home is in heaven. He tells us that we are just visitors on earth.

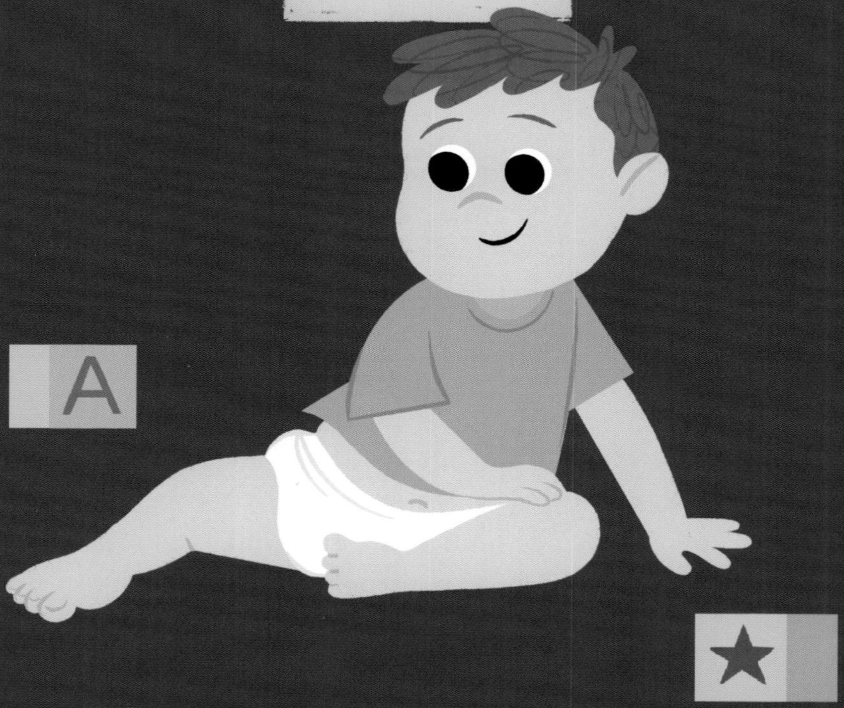

GRAMMY, SOMEBODY NEEDS HELP!

This weekend, we had two of our grandbabies over, Jami and Zach. We love to have them come because they live two hours away, and we don't see them as often as we'd like. Now, first let me explain how our crazy night in the basement got started. I hurt my back. Our mattress is too soft for my sore back. (Weird things happen to you when you get older.) So now Paul and I sleep on a hard air mattress in the basement.

Jami, our granddaughter, gets nervous, so she is right next to our air mattress. Zach is in a crib in our room too. I need to be able to hear him if he wakes up in the middle of the night. (You also can't hear well when you get older.)

Also our Hessid is with us. Where we go, she goes.

Never to be left behind is our pup, Anaiah. No puppy wants to be left alone.

So, all of us, are jammed into our one-room basement.

Jami woke up every hour to let us know that she needed the light on (the light never went out) or to find her blanket.

Every time Jami whimpered, Anaiah leapt up and scooted over to my face licking me as if to say, "Help Jami!" After reassuring Jami we were all fine, she went back to sleep and Anaiah did too.

Then Zach began crying. Zach was getting his fang teeth (those pointy ones), and they hurt when they grow in. Now Anaiah scooted over to Zach's crib, then ran back to me, licking my face as if to say, "Help Zach!"

Jami and Zach started taking turns. Jami's turn to cry. Zach's turn to cry. Jami's turn. Zach's turn.

Every time Jami and Zach cried, Anaiah dashed to their side. She knew they needed help, and she wasn't able to help them, but she was able to run to me and tell me with her whole body, "Hey, Grammy, wake up! Zach needs help." Or "Grammy, Jami is scared. Help her. I can't!" "Grammy, Grammy, check Jami!"

By the time the sun came up, Anaiah went down. She was pooped. When you care about people, you don't think about what you need. You are more concerned about others. That was Anaiah.

LUKE 9:23

Then [Jesus] said to all of them, "Whoever wants to follow me must say no to themselves. They must pick up their cross every day and follow me."

I WANT TO BE FIRST!

MATTHEW 19:30

Jesus says, "But many who are first will be last.
And many who are last will be first."

Anaiah always wants to be first. First out the door. First in the car. First to be fed. First to get a kiss. You name it, she wants to be first. But the first dog in our house isn't Anaiah. It's Hessid. Hessid is such a sweet Golden.

When I get up in the morning, I come down the steps and give Hessid a hug *first*. As I am giving Hessid her morning hug, Anaiah is crying to be let out of her crate. (She is in the crate because she eats big holes in our large, woven, wool rugs.) Once I come to Anaiah and open her crate, I give her a big old hug, and she in return gives me wet kisses.

As I make my cup of coffee, Hessid is still resting, and Anaiah is the first one in the toy basket. She always picks up the newest and funnest toy. After she has gotten her toy, she tosses it in the air, gives it a shake, gives it a shove and a good chomp, then remembers that she has to tinkle. Now Anaiah is the first to go to the door. When I open the door to let out both dogs, Anaiah is in the position of a racehorse at the starting gate. She is ready to leap out the door, leaving sweet Hessid with the door closing in on her.

After the dogs play outside, both of them come inside (guess who's first) to rest and relax while I read my Bible. This lasts about two hours for Hessid. It lasts two minutes for Anaiah.

Anaiah looks at me like, “What can we play now?” I tell her that after breakfast and chores we will go in the car to do errands.

Once my morning chores are finished, I tell the girls it is time to go. Anaiah has her nose pressed at the edge of the door, her back leg muscles tight and ready to leap. (Hessid has decided to wait at a safe distance.) On your mark, get set, open the door, and zoom! Anaiah leaps up into the back of my old car and comes to a vibrating stop. Meanwhile, Hessid lumbers to the car and carefully walks up a ramp that I have for her. (She has arthritis so jumping hurts.)

I started feeling bad for Hessid. So when I took Anaiah to her training class, I spoke with the trainer and asked her what I should do with the pup. Carol, the trainer, told me to make Anaiah sit and “wait,” and not let her be first. Only when I would give Anaiah a tap on the chest, would she be able to get up and go. Do you think this would work for Anaiah?

I am glad to tell you that it did! After *months* of working with Anaiah, she will now sit and wait at the door. She lets Hessid go first!

The Bible tells us to not be first. It actually tells us to be last. That is really hard to do. The trick is that we have to wait like Anaiah.

MY DAILY REMINDER

Sometimes while I am in the house and Paul is around, I'll hear a "bing" coming from his phone. When I ask about the bing, he usually tells me that it is to remind him of a meeting he has in thirty minutes. Those bings annoy me and are the reason I don't put my schedule on my phone!

But God has given me a big "bing"—a reminder that comes every day when I am on Mr. Beer's farm road. After about five minutes of a slow jog, I pass by what looks like lines of grass in the middle of the gravel, but the lines aren't grass; they are green wheat sprouts.

The farmer planted seeds not only in the field to the left, but he also accidentally planted some seeds on the gravel road.

Some of the seeds fell on the rocky soil, and other seeds fell on the good soil. Does that remind you of a story you've heard before?

Jesus saw a lot of food growing. He must have seen very heathy, green crops. But he also saw sick, dried-out, dying crops. Jesus lived where there were hot and dry seasons, like a desert. Could our hearts be like a garden that Jesus has planted seeds in? Seeds of love, joy, peace, patience, kindness, goodness, faithfulness, gentleness, and self-control. Just like seeds die from burning heat and no rain, could these seeds in my heart die when trouble comes and my love for him fades?

All of us have trouble. Jesus even says that in the Bible: "I have told you these things, so that you can have peace because of me. In this world you will have trouble. But be encouraged! I have won the battle over the world" (John 16:33).

So what do we do when trouble comes? Do we worry? Do we get mean? That is what kills the seed that God has planted in our hearts. God wants us to remember that he is faithful. God will always work everything together for good when we love and trust him.

So when I run on Mr. Beer's road tomorrow, I want to remember that God knows every single trouble that I am going to have, and that he will take care of me and work all these troubles out for good. What a great "bing"!

MATTHEW 13:3b–6

[Jesus] said, "A farmer went out to plant his seed. He scattered the seed on the ground. Some fell on a path. Birds came and ate it up. Some seed fell on rocky places, where there wasn't much soil. The plants came up quickly, because the soil wasn't deep. When the sun came up, it burned the plants. They dried up because they had no roots."

MATTHEW 6:8

"Your Father knows what you need even before you ask him."

Don't worry about anything. No matter what happens, tell God about everything. Ask and pray, and give thanks to him.

PHILIPPIANS 4:6

I AM WORRIED

Hessid did not want to eat the ground meat that I made for her this morning. That is kind of like Kim not wanting pizza on Friday night. Hessid took a walk with me this morning, but she didn't bounce like she usually does. Even as the hard rain blew into our faces, Hessid's pace was still slow.

We went to the vet yesterday, and as the vet gave Hessid a shot of antibiotic, she warned me that Hessid might feel even more sick with an upset tummy because of the shot. She was right.

When my animals get sick, I get worried.

I can do weird things when I worry. I can get really quiet. I can get busy with Windex and clean even clean things, and I can go "Google crazy," looking for answers to what I am worrying about. And I sigh a lot. I sigh so much that Paul can recognize my sighs and connect my sigh to my worry. Oh boy, that is a lot of sighing! None of this works.

But what does work is when I go to Jesus. Even before I tell him why I am worried, he already knows! (You can't hide anything from Jesus.) Not only does he know about it, but he cares about it. Jesus cares about what I am worrying about. To Jesus, nothing is small or unimportant. He made all things. Microscopic-small to telescopic-far!

Jesus wants me to tell him everything that is on my mind. He doesn't want me to worry because that will not help Hessid. Jesus wants me to pray for her, and he cares about her too.

"SWEETIE"

Hessid and I went into the vet's office. Hessid is eight years old, and in eight years, Hessid and I have been to the vet many times. The first thing we do is check in. Without a word from me, the receptionist says, "Hi Hessid! We're glad you're here. I'm sorry you don't feel well. Sit down, and we'll be with you soon."

Our favorite spot to sit is by the door. I sit on the bench, and Hessid is snuggled up to my left leg. Hessid and I try to sit as close as we can to the door because we like to see all the patients and their owners walk in. Puppies come in being held so tender by their proud new owner. Young dogs tend to enter yanking their owner through the doors at breakneck speed. Sometimes you will see young mothers maneuvering a stroller plus one or two preschoolers and a dog—all squeezing through the door at the same time! Hessid likes it when people come in holding pet carriers with "meows" resounding from the container. She tries to glance at who is making all that noise! Then there is always the dog that comes in and barks. And barks. And barks. With all of this going on, Hessid hasn't moved from my side.

The vet tech comes out, "Hessid, it's your turn." Off we go into the examining room. Hessid goes right onto the canine scale and stands still until the tech says, "105 pounds. Good girl. Dr. Walter will be with you soon."

Again I sit on the bench, and without a word, Hessid is at my left leg. We have never met Dr. Walter before. In a few moments, we are greeted with a handshake and quick introduction from Dr. Walter. Hessid glances at me and then proceeds to walk to Dr. Walter for her "Hello." Dr. Walter leads with a body rub, and Hessid greets with a sniff. Then Dr. Walters and I go on to discuss that Hessid is not eating and just not acting herself.

"What a sweetie," said Dr. Walter, and she continued to give Hessid her examination. "Yes. She sure is," I replied.

"What a special sweetness is in her. Just pours out of her," stated Dr. Walter. "Yes," I said.

How did Dr. Walter know Hessid was so sweet? She had just met her. Was it in the way Hessid let her pet her? Was it in Hessid's quietness? Was it in the way Hessid looked at Dr. Walter? Maybe it was all those things.

Dr. Walter finished her exam and gave Hessid a shot then a prescription for me to give to her for the next two weeks. With one more pet to Hessid and a handshake from me, we went back to the receptionist to pay the bill.

On my way to the car, I thought about Hessid's sweetness. She cannot talk, yet her sweetness is so vivid to people who meet her. Do people think I am sweet just by my presence? Does sweetness radiate out of me like it does Hessid?

Jesus, please help me radiate sweetness that comes from your presence in me.

PROVERBS 27:19 NLT

As a face is reflected in water, so the heart reflects the real person.

GOODBYE HESSID

ROMANS 8:21 NLT

The creation looks forward to the day when it will join God's children in glorious freedom from death and decay.

Hessid hasn't been eating well. She only eats liver and ground beef from my hand. Hessid hasn't been watching for the deer at night. She only wants to lie near me. Hessid didn't want to go on a walk, but she slowly went up the steps to sleep on her blanket next to my bed.

I took Hessid to the hospital because she was so sick. The vets thought she may get better if we started her on a medicine. We started the medicine. I called the vet hospital to see if I could come and visit her. They told me, "Sure. Come at 2:00." And I did.

I went into a small quiet room, and the nurse put a blanket on the floor for Hessid and me to sit and lie on. Then the nurse brought in Hessid. With her tail wagging and her big paws slowly walking over to me, she gave me a kiss. She told me that she loved me, and I told her that I loved her.

In a while, I noticed her breathing changed. Her big, brown eyes were very heavy as her panting got harder. I laid down next to her and told her it was going to be okay. Slowly, her head dropped into my cupped hands. I whispered in her big, warm, floppy ears that she was going to a place where her mommy was and to look for her mommy.

"Hessid, you're going to see mommy!" I whispered. Hessid died.

The nurses put Hessid in a box and covered her with a blanket, and I put her in the back of my car. She loved riding in the back of my car. It really isn't my car, but hers.

Mr. Beer came over with his backhoe and dug a hole for Hessid's body to go in. Before we put her in the ground, Kim, Paul, and I gave her our final kiss, and on the lid of her box, I put this:

"I know animals don't have souls, but I think they enter heaven on the coattails of their masters."

I can't wait to give Hessid another big old hug and kiss in heaven.

IT'S OKAY TO BE SAD

PSALM 34:18

The LORD is close to those whose hearts have been broken. He saves those whose spirits have been crushed.

It is morning, and Anaiah is sleeping in the exact spot Hessid used to sleep in, right on the floor, next to my bed. The alarm goes off and we wake up. Slowly Anaiah rolls over and gets up on her four paws. She rests her chin on the edge of the bed, as close to my face as she can. We look into each other's sad eyes for a few moments until I roll out of bed.

We both come downstairs. I make my coffee, and Anaiah finds her pillow bed and lies down again. I open up the door for Anaiah to go outside, but she only moves her eyebrows. Anaiah would have followed Hessid outside. Hessid was the leader. Without her leader, Anaiah is lost. So I put on my coat and coax Anaiah outside, and we look at the sunrise together. Everything is beautiful. The wheat is growing and so green. The birds are singing. The ground almost looks pink from the rising of the sun through the mist. But it just doesn't seem as beautiful as it was before.

I come back into the house with Anaiah following close behind. I sit and pray over the day. The day has the same chores that need to be done. But it is just harder to do them. The phone will ring with friends wanting to talk, but I don't feel like talking. I need to think about work, but I keep thinking about how different it was one week ago with Hessid right beside me. I look at Anaiah and say, "Jesus will help us today."

It can be hard to be with sad people because you get sad too. It is easy to share fun things and good things like candy and cake, but it is hard to share sadness. God shares our sadness.

Many times in the Bible when people were sad they prayed. God's ears are turned toward sad prayers. God cares about us. Sometimes when we are sad, we learn new things about God. Today I thought about God's quiet, unending love. He is never so busy that he doesn't have time to wait with me until I feel better. I don't need to tell God how I feel; he already knows. God loves me the way I am. Sad. Happy. Scared. Silly. It doesn't matter because his love is never-ending. Never-stopping. Never-quitting.

2 CORINTHIANS 1:4 NLT

He comforts us in all our troubles so that we can comfort others. When they are troubled, we will be able to give them the same comfort God has given us.

DONKEY HUGS

This morning, after I finished taking Anaiah out for her walk, we went to the barnyard. Anaiah use to sit on the porch with Hessid after our walks, but now she has found another spot to sit. She likes to sit at the gate to the pasture. There she can rub noses with the boys, and they enjoy each other's company.

With Anaiah sitting at the gate and the boys busy, I went about my morning routine. I swept off the goat shelves, cleaned up the poo, distributed animal crackers, and refilled two tubs with fresh water.

As I reached for the brush on the shelf, my mind started to wander again back to Hessid and how she loved getting brushed every day. The boys moseyed over to me, leaving Anaiah behind. They both like getting brushed. However, in the spring, they really enjoy getting those 350-pound, shedding, itchy bodies brushed. The brush to them feels like a back scratcher to me. After I finish brushing their bodies, I brush the inside of their ears. They have big ears! As they lean into the brush, I can almost hear them whisper, "Oh man, that feels so good. Thank you!"

Before leaving the boys, I stooped down to sweep up the last of the poo. As I swept, Kisses stood close to me. He put his neck over my back and carefully pulled me toward him with his chin, till my face was leaning against his side. Then Chuckie came to my other side. He got really close too. (I was a little scared that I was going to get squished.) Now Chuckie put his head over my back, and he gently pulled me close to him. I was getting a double donkey hug.

I know that they know I have been sad. This was their way to comfort me.

Jesus tells us to do that too. He tells us to comfort other people the way he comforts us.

ANAIAH AND THE BAD HABIT

Anaiah has a bad habit. (Actually she has more than one!) When Kim takes off her socks and puts them in the laundry, Anaiah will slink up to the laundry basket, lift her head slowly over the edge, take a deep whiff of smelly sock, and go for the grab.

When Paul takes off his sneakers and socks, Anaiah reaches her nose into the air to get a super whiff of smelly sock, and if the coast is clear, she grabs it!

Now, Anaiah knows this is not good dog behavior. If I happen to be standing next to her when she gets the smelly-sock whiff, she will muster up the self-control she needs to ignore the sock. But as soon as I'm not there, off she goes, clenching her little teeth onto the sock.

Once Anaiah gets the sock, she chews it. The same way that you chew a cheeseburger. She takes bites out of the sock then swallows it. Amazingly, Anaiah doesn't get sick from this. However, there are times you will find remnants of sock in her poo. Ugh! Disgusting!

When I catch Anaiah in the middle of eating a sock, I will tell her promptly to drop it. With that, she leaps into the air and springs backward. With a muffled bark, she tells me that she knows what she should do but doesn't want to. She wants to do what is right but just keeps doing what is wrong!

Time for me to get a treat—not to reward her—but to get her to drop the sock. This is a hard choice for Anaiah. She thinks, *I love this stinky sock, but I also love Grammy's cookies*. Now what? After I put down one more treat, Anaiah makes her choice. As she picks up her treats, I pick up the wet, stinky sock. But it's too late. I will see a piece of it in her poo tomorrow. Oh dear.

I am a lot like Anaiah. I start bad habits too. Jesus, please help Anaiah and I to get rid of our bad habits.

COLOSSIANS 3:9b

You have gotten rid of your old way of life and its habits.

"STAY"

PSALM 46:10a

"Be still and know that I am God."

Anaiah is still going to school. One of the things we do every week in class is to "stay." First, the dog trainer will tell us to get our dogs into position. This means I tell Anaiah, "Down." And most of the time, Anaiah goes down. Then the dog trainer tells us to "give the command." I respond by telling Anaiah, "Stay" and putting my hand in front of her face for a second. The last command the trainer gives is, "Leave your dog." I walk away from Anaiah. Then the trainer sets her timer. She sets it for five minutes.

Some of the dog owners leave their dog and go into a side room where their dogs cannot see them. Anaiah isn't up to that yet. Some owners stand right in front of their dog, ready to catch them if they "break the stay." Anaiah doesn't need me right in front of her. I am about the distance of two school buses away from her.

So you have about twelve dogs lined up against a wall all laying down on their bellies with their paws in front of them. You have big dogs, little dogs, old dogs, young dogs, and everything in between.

For the first minute of Anaiah's "stay," she stays. She is on her

belly and doesn't move. As the timer gets close to three minutes, she starts looking around at the other dogs. She might go from lying on her tummy to rolling onto her side. Sometimes her paw will hit the dog next to her. She wants to "party" and not be in a stay anymore. Then I will look at her and say, "Stay," and Anaiah will roll back onto her belly.

At four minutes, Anaiah starts with the army crawl. With her tummy on the floor, and her eyes on me, she shimmies, slowly, toward me. I tell her, "Stay," again. But this time it is just too much. She gets up on her paws and walks to me with her head down.

Everybody else is still lined up against the wall, but Anaiah just can't stay all five minutes.

I am a lot like Anaiah.

This morning when I woke up, I was so sad because I was thinking about Hessid. I just didn't want to get out of bed. I felt kind of sick in my tummy. How would I get through a busy day being so sad and thinking about Hessid? Jesus told me, "I will give you peace, if your mind stays on me."

I needed to stay thinking about Jesus and how good he was to give me Hessid. How good he was to give her good care. How good he was to give us eight fun years with her. I needed to stay. And just like I am filled with love watching Anaiah stay, Jesus is filled with even greater love watching me stay.

ANAIAH AND ME

1 CORINTHIANS 13:4b NLT

Love is not jealous or boastful or proud.

Anaiah and I do a lot of things together. In the morning, when the alarm goes off, I push the snooze button a few times and finally pull the warm covers off of my head. At the same time, Anaiah slowly stretches, creeps off of her pillow, and shakes her white, fluffy body. Our eyes meet, and we stand and come downstairs.

Once we're in the kitchen, I let Anaiah outside as I make my cup of coffee. When Anaiah is inside again, we read our Bible together. (Anaiah falls asleep with her head on my foot during this.) Then we exercise together. We eat together. When I go out to the barnyard, she is close by the fence watching every move I make. (She doesn't go into the barnyard because she would get brown and smell like poo.)

When I go to the grocery store, she gets in the car with me. (She loves the car!) When I visit my mom in the nursing facility, Anaiah comes with me and greets everyone she meets like they are her best buddy.

God made dogs, and he made them to live together in a pack. So when Anaiah sees me, she sees me as part of her pack! That's kind of funny because I don't have fur, floppy ears, a tail, or a wet nose—but to her, I am part of her pack.

Last night after dinner, Paul came over to give me a hug. (He always gives me a hug after dinner!) Of course, Anaiah was sitting right next to me. She got down on her tummy with her bottom in the air and started to bark. Paul wondered what she was barking at. I said, “Anaiah’s jealous!”

“Of whom?” Paul asked.

“Of you hugging me!” I stated.

Paul didn’t quite believe me so he hugged me again, and sure enough Anaiah let out a big, old bark with her tail wagging, looking right at us. Paul had his proof. Anaiah was jealous of us hugging each other.

How many times do I get jealous? Sometimes it is little things I see someone else has, that I want. Like our neighbors’ barn doors that aren’t all chewed up!

Sometimes it’s bigger things. I remember when I was in school, it was hard for me to see kids get better grades than me, especially when I worked harder than them.

I guess Anaiah isn’t the only one who gets jealous!

ONE SMALL THING

Berachah's name comes from the Hebrew language and means "blessing." I got her when she was eight weeks old, along with two other pygmy goats, Nuah and Getty.

Berachah has always had a lot of spunk and is a bit on the nervous side. She bounces from rock to rock in our pasture and flies up the ladder to her "spot" on the shelf in the barn. Berachah lays on the left side of the shelf, and Nuah lays on the right side.

One day, I noticed that Berachah didn't finish her grain at breakfast. That's okay because there are many times and reasons animals might not finish a meal. But over the next few days, Berachah ate less and less, until she wasn't eating at all.

At the same time, I also noticed that Berachah wasn't hanging out with the boys or the other goats. She was hiding in the barn. Her bright, big eyes looked sick. She didn't have her pep.

A few days later, as I was cleaning up the barn, Nuah wanted to play with Berachah and gave her a butt, but Berachah fell down. I knew something was wrong. Berachah was sick, so I called the vet.

The vet came over in his truck and listened to Berachah's heart and her breathing. (Just like when you go to your doctor.) Dr. Arlan, the vet, thought she had an infection in her lungs, so he put her on an antibiotic to clear it up. The vet also said that she was anemic. That means that you don't have enough red cells in your blood. When you are anemic, you are weak and very tired. So the vet gave Berachah a shot of iron to help her anemia.

A few days later, Berachah was no better. She was even more weak. And now I could see how skinny she was.

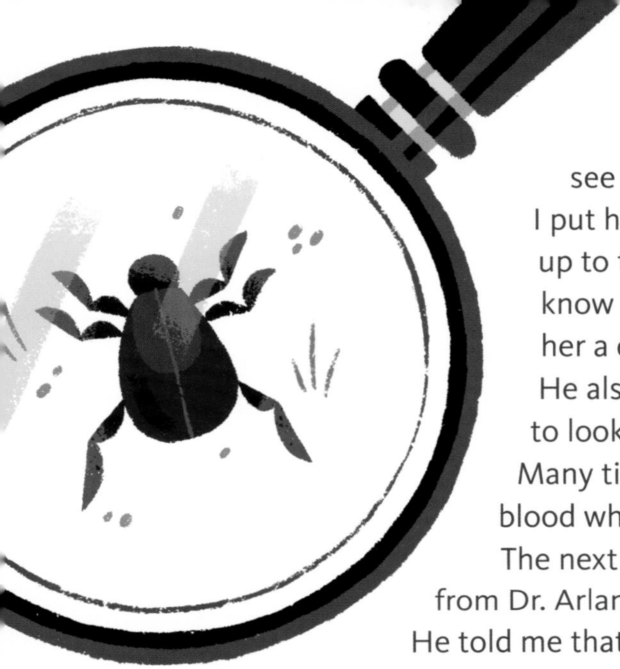

I could tell she needed to see the vet again. So this time, I put her in my car, and we drove up to the vet. Dr. Arlan didn't know what to do. So he gave her a different kind of antibiotic. He also took some of her blood to look at under a microscope. Many times you can see from blood what might be wrong.

The next morning I got a phone call from Dr. Arlan.

He told me that Berachah had a tick bite, and from that bite, a parasite was eating Berachah's white blood cells. So now Berachah needed one shot a day of an antibiotic for twenty-one days.

How could something so small—a parasite that could only be seen with a microscope—hurt Berachah so much?

Berachah had the tick bite for a month or two before I noticed how it was hurting her. The bacteria started so slow and hidden, but it could kill her.

Sin is like that. It can start hidden. No one knows about it but you and God. And then the sin takes over. Slowly it takes over your body, and it can destroy you.

Jesus is the great Healer and Forgiver of our sin. When we confess it, Jesus forgives it. He doesn't even want to remember our sin anymore.

1 JOHN 1:9

But God is faithful and fair. If we confess our sins, he will forgive our sins. He will forgive every wrong thing we have done. He will make us pure.

THE GOLDEN RULE

The birds woke me up this morning. I had missed that during the winter. The quiet and darkness of winter has gone away! Now we wake up to a pink, purplish sky, with the sun slowly peeking over the horizon. I love to wake up to the sun rising. After crawling out of bed, I gave Anaiah her belly rub, along with a "Good morning."

After a few minutes, with a cup of coffee in my tummy, I go out to my friends. It is so good to see Berachah being brave and strong enough to gingerly climb up the ladder to her spot on the shelf! It has been almost three months that her spot has been empty. Thank you, Jesus, that today she is a bit stronger.

The goats eagerly gobble down their grain and chomp on their carrots. All heads are turned to me, eyes staring, waiting for their one animal cracker. (I say "one" because everyone is a bit chubby, except for little Berachah.)

Now I climb over the fence to those sweet boys who are waiting patiently. They check out the carrots that I pull out of my sweatshirt pocket. After a good sniff, the carrot passed the test. What's the test? If my hands smell like Anaiah, then the carrots will smell like Anaiah, and if the carrots smell like Anaiah, they won't eat the carrot! Today I had made sure I washed my hands before I grabbed the carrots, so they passed the sniff test and went down the hatch.

Time to grab the brush. The boys love to get brushed, especially in the spring. Now is the time their coats are shedding from the long, cold winter. I start with Kisses. He leans into the brush and gently moves his body to get the most of my strokes against his thick, gray fur. The climax of the brushing is when I brush the inside of their long, furry ears. They *love* that! As I finish brushing Kisses, Chuckie moves right into place. He's waited patiently, watching me as I brushed his brother. He wants his turn! So I repeat the same strokes with Chuckie.

After finishing the brushing, I went to pick up the poo. The goats are watching every move I make. (I think they are praying they get more cookies!) But the boys are just standing next to one another. All of a sudden, Chuckie slowly and gently reaches over and scratches Kisses back with soft chews from his big teeth. At the same time, Kisses reaches over and chews Chuckie's back with his teeth.

The boys are following the golden rule! Do unto others as you want to be done to you!

Jesus told us to follow the golden rule. If I want my back scratched, I will scratch my best friend's back!

LUKE 6:31

Do to others as you want them to do to you.

JAMES 3:17

But the wisdom that comes from heaven is pure. That's the most important thing about it. And that's not all. It also loves peace. It thinks about others. It obeys. It is full of mercy and good fruit. It is fair. It doesn't pretend to be what it is not.

ARE YOU WISE AS A GOAT?

Have you ever heard the expression "as wise as an owl"? I have another creature to add to the list of being wise.

Last week, I saw Berachah stand on her favorite rock! I hadn't seen her do that for two months because she had been so sick from the tick bite. From the top of the rock, she quickly glanced around to see if the coast was clear. No other goats were around. Off she jumped from her rock to the smaller rock! On no, she fell off. Now, remember that God has made goats so agile that they climb up cliffs that are almost vertical (straight up and down)—so to fall from one rock to another is a huge blow even for Berachah.

But this week, Berachah was brave enough to try the same jump again. And she did it! After this accomplishment, I noticed Nuah, her buddy, joining her back on her favorite rock. Nuah gently gave her a rub with her nose. I think she was saying in goat body language, "That was great Berachah!" The two of them spent the next few minutes gently playing and resting on each other.

Months before this, you would have seen Nuah and Berachah running, butting, and chasing one another all over the goat house, doing 360-degree spins in the air, delighting in each other.

But now you see the beauty of their friendship displayed in gentleness. Sometimes it can be difficult to be gentle, especially if you are used to playing hard every day.

So if you hear someone use the expression "as wise as an owl," you can add to it "as wise as a goat!"

ENDING UP WHERE YOU DON'T BELONG!

PROVERBS 12:26

Godly people are careful about the friends they choose.
But the way of sinners leads them down the wrong path.

This morning, I woke up and heard a different sound from the barnyard. I looked out the window as the sun was coming up, and I saw Edith on the ramp. Poor Edith. I put on my sneaks and went out to see what was going on.

From the looks of it, I think Edith was stuck on the ramp almost all night. As I picked her up (which is no small feat because she weighs about 100 pounds), I could tell that she was wet from sweating. There was a lot of poo and tinkle on the ramp, so Edith had been stuck for quite a while—maybe even all night. (As a matter of fact, I think I heard her during the night, and I thought it was a kit, a baby fox, calling for its mommy.)

Why was Edith stuck? Well, you see, Edith is a fainting goat, and when she gets scared, she gets so stiff that she "freezes" and can't move. When this happens on the ground, she will just fall over. But this time, she knew if she fell over she would fall off the ramp, so she just froze—kind of like when you play freeze tag.

Why did Edith go on the ramp? Well, Nuah and Berachah run up and down the ramps like you run up and down your stairs. Edith saw them having so much fun, she thought she would join in. But God didn't make Edith like he made Nuah and Berachah. She should not have followed them up the ramp.

Do you ever follow people whom you shouldn't then "freeze," thinking, *I shouldn't be here!* Do you try to fit in and be like other kids (Get it? Goats are called kids!), and it just doesn't work?

I think each of us has found ourselves at a place we shouldn't be, and followed kids we shouldn't follow, then we get that "stuck" feeling. But just like I saw Edith, and I came running, we should call to Jesus, and he will come running to help us. (Jesus's ears are much better than mine, so he can hear us even during the night.)

Do you think Edith will do this again? I hope not. And I hope that you and I remember this when we get stuck trying to be like other kids.

HIDDEN BUT DEADLY

Some people say that they have only done one small thing that was wrong. I have said that. How can something bad happen from one small thing?

That is what happened to Berachah. One small tick bit her. We don't know when—it could have been a long time ago. How can a tiny tick, that is the size of a pin head, hurt a young, healthy goat? How can something so small hurt a big goat?

Three weeks after giving Berachah all thirty shots, the sickness came back. One morning she slowly climbed up the ladder to the top shelf. She quickly gazed around to make sure none of the other goats were near her to push her off. She gently took one mini carrot from my hand. Chomp. Chomp. Chomp. She tried to take a second, but she just didn't feel like it and spit it out.

While I was cleaning up the barn, she watched me rake. I told her how glad I was that the sun was shining. At that clue, Berachah gingerly walked down the ladder, that months ago she had charged up and down. She walked out to her patch on the field. Gently, she pawed at the ground and carefully crouched down to lay in the rays of the warm, spring sun that she had longed for all winter.

After finishing the cleanup, I came into the house to work. Each time I passed the window, I peeked out to make sure Berachah was okay.

How could a small tick do this? I wondered. *How can something so small destroy her? Can something small hurt me?*

One small thing I do that hurts me is worrying. Many times they are not big worries but small ones. My worries are like the tick bite on Berachah. They start out so small that no one sees them. But after days, weeks, or even months of worrying, my face changes from a happy face to a sad face. My good night's sleep is interrupted a lot, and I look exhausted. When I am exhausted, I can get mean. When I am mean, I can say things that aren't kind. Then I hurt the people whom I love with icky, mean words.

That same night, Berachah died. Because of that one small tick bite.

Jesus died for all of my sins. Big ones and small ones. And some day, God is going to make a new heaven and a new earth. There will be no small (or big) things that will hurt us anymore. I hope to see Berachah jumping from rock to rock along the river that runs from the throne of God.

Thank you, Jesus. Thank you, God.

REVELATION 21:1a

I saw a "new heaven and a new earth."
The first heaven and the first earth were completely gone.

—CHAPTER 32—

SHAKE, RATTLE, AND ROLL

PSALM 91:2

I will say about the LORD, "He is my place of safety. He is like a fort to me. He is my God. I trust in him."

It is so wonderful to hear the sounds of spring. The high-pitched tweets coming from the straw- filled birdhouse. Mr. Beer's diesel tractor as it barrels up and down the fields breaking up the hard ground. Then there is the pinging of lawn mowers. With the spring grass growing so quickly, everybody is on mowers. Kids. Parents. Grandparents. I've even seen a dog on a mower!

Now there is another sound that we hear in spring. It starts with Anaiah's tags on her collar jiggling. Then the radio gets crackly. Clouds begin to swirl and darken. Anaiah at this point stands so close to me that I can't move! And . . . a roll of distant thunder.

Anaiah looks up at me as if to say, "Grammy, the world is coming to an end." I assure Anaiah, "We will be fine."

Anaiah's eyes widen. Her breathing is so loud that I can't hear anything else. In my head I rehearse what the vet says: "Just keep doing what you are doing and ignore Anaiah during the storm." That does not work.

But I have found something that does work. A *Thundershirt*! This is a special shirt that wraps tightly around an animal, making them feel like they are being hugged. Before a storm comes, I put a Thundershirt on Anaiah, and I can't hear her breathe, and her eyes don't look like they are going to pop out of her head. She is wrapped up tight and feels safe.

It reminds me how Jesus holds me tight, and I am safe in his arms.

CLOTHED IN CASHMERE

How wonderful! The grass is green. The birds are singing. Spring is in the air. And that is not the only thing in the air. As I walk out to my friends, I notice fluffy hairballs floating in the air and rolling on the ground. Yes, this is another sign of spring!

I don't have any grain with me because my friends have an entire field of fresh grass to chew on all day long. But all the animals still waddle up to me anticipating the animal crackers

that will be coming out of my sweatshirt pocket. They all love animal crackers! Everybody gets two of them.

As Chezlee walks up to me, I see clumps of fur hanging off both of his horns. Since goats don't have fingers to scratch their skin, they use the tips of their horns. When the goats give themselves a good itch, the fur comes off their bodies and sticks to their horns. Also, to help the goats get a good scratch, Paul has nailed scrubbing brushes to the corners of the barn. The goats and donkeys will rub their entire bodies along the brushes—starting with the face and ending with the butt—and oh that feels so good to them!

When I see the fur on the goat horns, in the brushes, and whirling through the air and on the ground, it reminds me of how much God protected and provided for each one of them during the winter. As a matter of fact, the coat God put on the goats is way more expensive than the winter coat I put on myself! God has given the goats coats made of cashmere. Cashmere is a soft, downy wool that is very expensive. If I want to buy a coat made of cashmere, it could cost me a thousand dollars. And to think God puts that on goats!

Now if God provides for Chezlee, Edith, Getty, Nuah, and Berachah, won't he provide for you and me? He sure will.

MATTHEW 6:28–30

"And why do you worry about clothes? See how the wild flowers grow. They don't work or make clothing. But here is what I tell you. Not even Solomon in all his royal robes was dressed like one of these flowers. If that is how God dresses the wild grass, won't he dress you even better? Your faith is so small! After all, the grass is here only today. Tomorrow it is thrown into the fire."

A KERNEL OF CORN

MICAH 7:14a

LORD, be like a shepherd to your people. Take good care of them.

This morning I met our neighbor, Mr. Beer, on the road. He was checking on his corn because we haven't had much rain. I asked him about the tassels on the top of the corn. They look like little pom-poms on the top of each stalk. I asked Mr. Beer if the corn continued to grow after the tassels were coming out the top of the stalks.

"Not much after that," Mr. Beer answered. "Do you want to know something about corn, Jill?" "Sure!" I said.

"Every kernel of corn has a piece of silk attached to it with the other end of the silk making up the tassel. [This is the silky stuff you pick off your corn before you put the butter on it.] If there

are one hundred kernels of corn on the cob, there will be one hundred strands of silk to pollinate, or feed, the kernel and make up the tassel. If a kernel has no silk, it won't grow. That is why some kernels are missing on stalks of corn. When the temperature gets over ninety degrees, it is hard for the silk to pollinate the kernel."

On my way back to the house, I said to myself, "Wow! That is really neat, God. You're amazing! You throw stars into the sky and name them. You feed kernels of corn! You do great big things, and you do small tiny things."

Opening the door to the kitchen, I noticed the long list of things that I had written down that morning. Things I had to do and things I was worried about. People say making lists helps you with worry. Well, our God did something much better for me and my worried heart than making a list. I saw God taking care of one kernel of corn that will be gobbled up. Can you imagine how he will take care of each one of us, his kids, whom he loves so much?

PLAYTIME!

PSALM 104:26

Ships sail back and forth on it.
Leviathan, the sea monster you made, plays in it.

In the center of the field is a bright red ball. It has a red handle attached to it. If you walk toward the barn, you might spot a purple tug toy woven through the grass. Shredded, multicolored rope toys scatter the field. And there is the large, rubber, red Frisbee.

As neighbors take their daily walk up and down our street, they stop. Chuckie and Kisses have their teeth at either end of the purple tug toy. They are dragging each other all the way around the field! Not just once but many times around. No wonder the neighbors stop to look and laugh. The boys look like two three-hundred-pound dogs playing wildly with one another. Sometimes the boys will get so riled up that they leave the toys behind and just pull on each other. Kisses will pull Chuckie by the ears, then Chuckie will grab Kisses's leg, and Kisses will hop around while chewing on Chuckie's neck. They are playing. And they love to play!

When the boys are playing, the goats don't want to be left out either. We have two boulders in the field, next to a large wooden spool that used to hold cable. The goats play "king of the mountain"—butting each other on and off the rocks and onto the wooden spool. This is the game of choice! Then the goats play tag with everyone scooting in and out of the barn and up and down the ladders at breakneck speed. Sometimes when I look out my kitchen window, it looks like a recess yard, except instead of kids, it's real kids!

Now the chain of fun has begun. When the boys get riled up, the goats get riled up. And then the dogs get riled up. Everyone is riled! Chasing, pulling, playing!

God loves it when we take time to play and enjoy one another and him. That is how he has made us: for praise *and* play!

PSALM 32:8 NLT

The LORD says, "I will guide you along the best pathway for your life. I will advise you and watch over you."

STAY ON THE PATH

A few months ago, I looked for our house on Google Maps, and I found it. I also found the tribe's house! Zooming in, I even saw the paths the boys have made in the field.

Many times, when I go outside to clean the small barn in the morning, the boys are grazing at the other end of the field. As soon as they see me, they "taste" a treat. The quickest way to get to me would be coming straight toward me. But the boys zigzag back and forth, way out of the way, and follow their path to me. This path goes all the way around and takes a long time. But the boys always stay on this path. They will graze off of the path, but when they move in a hurry, it is always on the path.

Mr. Beer, the farmer, told me that animals like to run on paths because they know that they are safe. There are no rocks or small stones hidden by grass on the path. The boys are surefooted, and they want to know that each step is safe. Staying on the path is the safe way for them to come to me.

As a matter of fact, in the winter, when the field is covered with snow, the boys will stay in the barn. They will stay in there as long as there is snow. All January and February, they just stand there at the door. They both have their big heads tilted down, and they look so sad. Why do they stay in the barn? They stay there because the pasture is covered with snow, and they can't see the ground.

Staying on the path is safe for them.

Jesus says the same thing to us. He has made a path for us to stay on. When we walk or run on his path, we are safe too.

AUGUST MORNING

PSALM 63:7

Because you have helped me, I sing in the shadow of your wings.

You know it is August when the sun beams into your tanned skin, when your skin is slippery from sweat, and when you hear crickets chirping louder than the birds. You also know it is August when I take Anaiah out early for her walk before it gets blazing hot. Most of the time we are successful but unfortunately not this morning!

This morning we woke up to the carpenter coming to fix the barn. He was replacing the boards that the boys had chewed up. After I explained to Matt, the carpenter, how to donkey-proof the door (you cover up all the edges of the door with metal strips), the August sun was up in the sky.

Coming back into the house after talking with Matt, I got Anaiah's leash on, and we were on our way. She started out fine, "healing" as she was taught to do in her puppy obedience classes. But after about five minutes, I saw her lagging a bit. Now, most of the time when Anaiah gets tired, she slowly gets farther and farther behind me, but today was different. She stayed to my left, lagging slightly behind me. Anaiah is so smart! She was staying in my shadow. She was hidden from the blazing sun. I was protecting her. I was protecting her from the sun's heat.

I couldn't help but test her out. When I went faster, she went faster. When I went slower, she went slower. When I stopped, she stopped. All Anaiah had to do was focus on me, and in my shadow she had a grand old time on her walk! I was the one who got all the sunshine. She was the one who got all the shade.

Jesus is like that. He walks so closely to us, that he is able to protect us too. All we need is to stay in his shadow and enjoy our walk!

SOMEBODY'S KNOCKING AT MY DOOR

Anaiah and I were just coming in from our early morning walk. We were able to get out early enough to beat the sun rising over the corn. That means Anaiah's tongue wasn't hanging out too far by the time we got back home!

When we jumped up our porch steps, I noticed that someone was knocking at our door. I couldn't tell if it was a male or female. It was definitely strong. It could have been a gymnast. All four of its appendages, or legs, were holding onto the frame of the door. It had bumpy skin. And it was green except for the orangish suction cups at the end of its toes.

If I opened the door, where would this creature go? Yikes! Anaiah hadn't noticed the guest at the door yet, but if she did, I knew it would be trouble. Trouble with a capital T! Thankfully all Anaiah wanted to do was come into the house and get a big drink of cool water.

So slowly, very slowly I opened the door. Our new friend continued to hang onto the door frame. As I was filling Anaiah's bowl with fresh water, she stayed perched on the mat outside, right under our friend, looking through the screen to make sure I was getting her a drink. I waited for her to bark. No bark.

Opening the door again, very gingerly, our friend was still sucked onto the wood. However, as I put down Anaiah's bowl, I noticed movement from the frame to the screen. I was surprised the suction cups held onto screening.

As soon as Anaiah had a good, long drink, she laid down on the mat, perfectly positioned under our friend. Not a bark.

In the Bible, it says that our hearts are like a door. And someone is standing outside our heart knocking on the door. He is Jesus. He is knocking to come into our hearts and into our lives. But there is no doorknob on the outside of this door. The only way Jesus can come in is if we open up our door from the inside and invite him in. Some people are like Anaiah—they don't even notice that someone is at the door of their heart. I hope you notice Jesus knocking today. I hope you invite him in. And once Jesus comes into your heart, he begins to make you more and more like himself—glorious!

REVELATION 3:20a

"Here I am! I stand at the door and knock.
If anyone hears my voice and opens the door, I will come in."

— CHAPTER 39 —

"PEPPER POPPERS"

PSALM 84:11b NLT

The LORD will withhold no good thing from those who do what is right.

Every day when I go out to the barnyard, Chuckie and Kisses, Edith, Chezlee, Nuah, and Getty are anxiously waiting for the goodies I bring to them. Today was no exception. I had all five bowls full of goat grain. But this morning, I had no carrots and no "Pepper Poppers" for Chuckie and Kisses. Pepper Poppers are a special treat—like peppermint candy for donkeys.

Just yesterday, I noticed that Chuckie was tiptoeing. *Oh no!* I said to myself. *Chuckie is beginning to founder again.* Foundering is when a donkey gets too much sugar into their bodies. Somehow the sugar hurts their feet. When you or I eat too much sugar, it can hurt our teeth; but not the boys, their feet start to hurt. Their feet can get so sore that they can lose the nail on their hooves—and it hurts a lot.

You might be wondering how they get sugar. Sugar is in fresh green grass; sugar is in fruit and vegetables, like carrots; and they can get sugar from their Pepper Poppers.

So this morning, I was Pepper-Popper free.

I gave the goats their grain in their usual feeding spots. Chezlee and Edith go on one side of the barn. Getty has her own secluded spot so she can eat in peace, and the baby goats eat on the top shelf.

After feeding the goats, I then proceed to sweep up the poo. And there can be a lot of poo from only five little goats and two sweet donkeys. As I sweep up the donkey poo, Chuckie and Kisses come over and give me a nudge. They love to be close, and I love to pet them.

After I clean up the poo, I always brush the boys. They love me to gently brush the inside of their ears. I think their ears get a little itchy, and it must feel so good as they lean into the coarse bristles of the brush.

After the brushing comes the clean water. Every day. Fresh water.

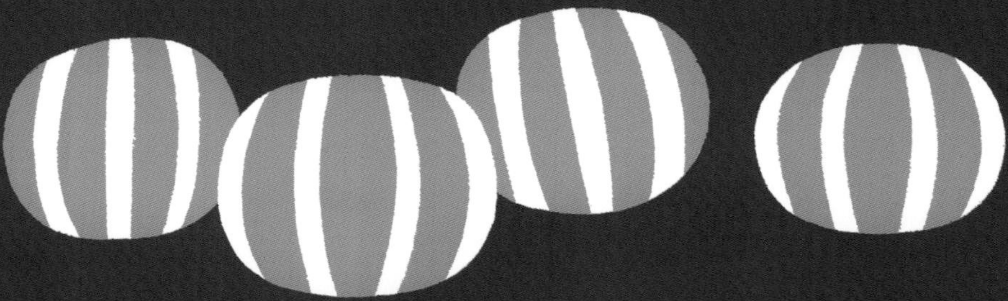

After the water, the Pepper Poppers come out. But not today! No Pepper Poppers from Grammy today. Chuckie and Kisses look at me, expecting me to pull out their favorite treats. I see their big eyes looking so deep into mine, looking for a sign of me reaching into my pocket for the Pepper Poppers. I hear a very quiet bray asking for the Pepper Poppers. I feel awful that I can't give them their favorite treat. If I do, it will hurt Chuckie. I try to explain the situation to the boys, but all they do is reach into my sweatshirt pocket and come up with shreds of old hay.

The boys know I love them. If I could only explain why I can't give them what they are expecting and wanting.

God is like that. He is my father. He loves me more than I love the boys. God has said that he will always give me everything I need—but maybe what I am asking for is not the best for me right now. God knows just the perfect time to reach into his "pocket" to pull out what I have been asking him for. God will not keep any good thing from me.

—CHAPTER 40—

THE GEESE

The boys came to greet me this morning (and every morning) by the gate, sniffing to see if I remembered their carrots. They love the smell of the carrots, but they do not like the smell of Anaiah and Tully on my hands! The goats are anxiously grabbing the soft, red leaves that have fallen between the fencing. My rubber boots sink into the mud, and I walk over to the radio. I always turn on the radio in the mornings to hear people talk about Jesus. I wonder if the animals listen.

This morning on the radio, the man was talking about heaven—my favorite subject! Wow. The man said, "If we knew how wonderful heaven really was, we wouldn't look both ways before we crossed the street!" I laughed at that one. "God will be always making everything new." I love new things. I like how clean they look and how they smell. I thought of how I will see Pop-Pop and Ben and Aunt Barbara. How they will look in their new bodies.

I was thinking of how I will be able to see Jesus's face whenever I want to—and I will be able to ask him questions.

Then I heard honking. Not from a car but from the sky. Not right over my head but in the distance. Canadian geese. So many that I couldn't count them making a huge *V* in the sky. The boys looked up, and the goats stopped eating the leaves, as the honks got louder and louder. The goose at the tip of the *V* was constantly changing direction with his friends following, like a dance. There was no competition. The geese were aware of one another, staying together, supporting one another, and bound for one destination. And they flew with determination.

God, please help me today to remember that my destination is heaven. Help me to "fly" today with determination, loving and caring for the people whom you put around me. Thank you that you are at the tip of our *V* and you lead us perfectly. I love you.

PHILIPPIANS 3:20

But we are citizens of heaven. And we can hardly wait for a Savior from there. He is the Lord Jesus Christ.

SOARING!

Have you ever thought about flying? As a kid, I remember wishing I could fly to school. What would it feel like?

God knows how much we would love to fly. In fact, in the Bible, God talks about us *soaring*. What does it mean to soar? It means to fly like an eagle!

Not just any animal can soar. God made the body of an eagle light enough to fly but still very strong. It has to be light, so it can fly high, but strong enough to dive down and grab its dinner! God made the bones of the eagle hollow—which means that only air is inside most of their bones. That's what makes them so light. But what God made heavier in eagles was their muscles. They use the muscles in their wings a lot!

The eagle's wings control speed kind of like a car's gas pedal. Eagles fly faster when their wings are up, and slower when their wings are down. They also brake with their wings—which helps them grab their food on the run!

When an eagle first takes off, it will flap its wings. But once up, it soars; it flies without flapping its wings. You see, the air pushes the wings so perfectly that the eagle only has to keep its wings in a position for the air to move it along. This is soaring. The eagle can fly two to four hours without landing!

The mommy eagle is bigger than the daddy eagle, and her wings are eight feet wide when she is flying. But her wings only weigh two pounds! How did God create this majestic bird that its wings are even stronger than airplane wings, yet so light?!

Sometimes eagles will play and do tricks in the air, kind of like the Blue Angels! (They are Navy pilots who perform special tricks in planes at air shows.) Eagles can dive down two hundred miles per hour! They play by doing somersaults over and over in the air then lock their claws together and spiral down thousands of feet.

Think about how God perfectly designed this majestic bird to soar! And the Bible says that those who trust in God will soar high on wings like eagles. Don't you think that the same God who designed the wings and body of this bird knows how to give you strength when you trust in him?

Why did our God make such a majestic, fun bird? All for his glory.

ISAIAH 40:31

But those who trust in the LORD will receive new strength. They will fly as high as eagles. They will run and not get tired. They will walk and not grow weak.

1 CORINTHIANS 10:13
You are tempted in the same way all other human beings are. God is faithful. He will not let you be tempted any more than you can take. But when you are tempted, God will give you a way out. Then you will be able to deal with it.

CHAPTER 42

THE ASH TREES

Last fall, I was driving on a local road. I love this street in the fall because the ash trees stand close together and the limbs reach out over the street like a canopy. The colors are just stunning!

As I turned the corner, something was different. Nearly all the beautiful trees had been chopped down and were lying along the side of the road.

There is a bug called the emerald ash borer that destroys ash trees. This is exactly what happened to the trees on my favorite street. How can a small bug kill such a mighty tree?

The adult emerald ash borer starts by eating the leaves on the ash tree. Then the female lays eggs in the cracks of the bark.

In two weeks, the eggs hatch into larvae. The larvae chew through the bark and make *J*-shaped tunnels deep in the tree. These *J* shapes destroy how the tree gets water and nutrients, so then the tree dies.

Then the larvae turn into an adult, and they chew holes from the tunnel right back through the bark and make an exit hole.

Sin is like this bug. It lands in my soul, or heart, and before I know it, I feel so far from Jesus. Some sin starts out quite small and invisible. No one can see it, but it wiggles in and can wreck me.

Oh how I need Jesus—every day!

Jesus, please help me be aware of the stuff that can wiggle deep into my heart and ruin my friendship with you.

NOT A GOOD WAY TO START THE DAY

PSALM 121:6

The sun won't harm you during the day.
The moon won't harm you during the night.

It was a beautiful summer morning, and it started like any other, with a cup of coffee and reading the Bible. After eating breakfast, doing a slow jog, and walking Anaiah and Tully, it was time to go out to the barnyard.

Chuckie and Kisses, my donkeys, were ready to greet me, and even more ready to grab the apples from my sweatshirt pocket! And the goats were telling me with their bleats that they were hungry too.

I got the rake and started cleaning up after the boys. Then I hopped over the fence to start cleaning and feeding the goats. As I reached down to open the bag of grain, I saw it!

A snake! It wasn't a garden snake; it was a copperhead. Oh my! Paul was home, but I didn't want to leave the animals with the snake. I was afraid the copperhead could hurt them. I was also afraid that the snake could slither away and come back when I wasn't there and hurt the animals. I couldn't be with them day and night.

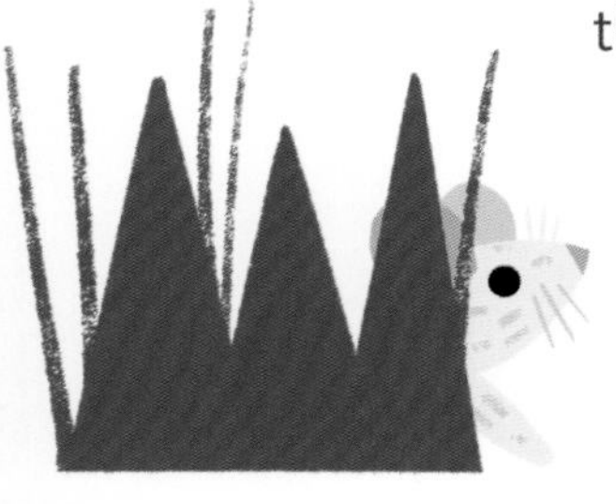

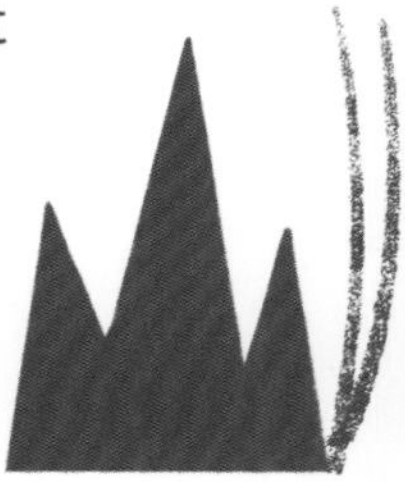

What should I do? I thought.

Breathing kind of heavy because I hate snakes and didn't know what to do, I looked around for a way to kill it.

I saw a shovel. It was the kind of shovel that has a flat top.

I took the shovel off the wall, walked over to the snake, and hit it as hard as I could. As soon as I killed it, I dropped the shovel, ran out of the barn, let out a scream, and jumped up and down because I was so grossed out!

All this time, the animals were watching me the way you watch TV. They were staring. They didn't have a clue how badly this snake could hurt them, but I did.

Sometimes I don't have a clue how the devil wants to hurt me, but Jesus does. And Jesus is so big, so strong, and so mighty that he can protect me way more than I can protect the boys and goats!

HE'S WATCHING

I saw Chezlee's sides moving in and out. *Really* in and *really* out. I could tell his heart was beating fast. Remember, when Chezlee gets scared or is really happy, he faints! (If you look up "fainting goats" on YouTube, you can see how they actually faint.) I called the vet. When I told the vet how Chezlee was acting, he thought Chezlee could have a blockage in his urinary track that was preventing him from peeing. I needed to get Chezlee to the vet as quickly as I could. So, Paul and I lifted Chezlee into the back seat, and I headed off. Once we got there, it was hard to get Chezlee out because he "froze" (he's a fainting goat and that's what they do). His front legs got stuck under the front seat. Poor guy.

When the vet saw Chezlee, he confirmed what was wrong. Chezlee couldn't pee because there was a stone in the way. Now this isn't like a stone we find in the ground but a ball of minerals that form a stone shape.

In about an hour, they operated on Chezlee and removed the stones. Not one but a few. The vet reported that he did well and would stay overnight just to make sure he would continue tinkling.

When I picked up Chezlee the next morning, the vet commented, "It's really good that you got him here so fast and that you saw him in pain. A lot of goats don't make it." And I thought to myself, "It's a really good thing that God had me in the barn with Kim and her buddies so I could see Chezlee in pain."

I notice goats. And God notices goats. Jesus says in Matthew 6:25–26 that God notices birds and takes care of them. So I'm sure he knew Chezlee needed help! I am probably one of the few people who notice goats in the Bible—but they are in there! Like in the story about the man named Job. He suffered so much. He lost everything he owned, including his children. At one point he asked God, "Do you know about me? Why did all this happen to me?"

See how God answered Job in the verses below. And remember, if God notices mountain goats, don't you think he sees us? Chezlee was such a reminder to me that if God cares about a sweet, old goat, he cares much more about you and me! Our God is an awesome God!

JOB 39:1–4a

"Job, do you know when mountain goats have their babies? Do you watch when female deer give birth? Do you count the months until the animals have their babies? Do you know the time when they give birth? They bend their back legs and have their babies. Then their labor pains stop. Their little ones grow strong and healthy in the wild."

POWERFUL!

EPHESIANS 3:16

I pray that he will use his glorious riches to make you strong.
May his Holy Spirit give you his power deep down inside you.

This morning, Kim and I were walking on Mr. Beer's farm road. I usually walk in front of Kim with Tully on my left and Anaiah on my right. A few steps behind me, Kim is signing along to songs that are coming from my phone in her jacket pocket.

Kim enjoys her music. I enjoy walking the pups. We both enjoy the view. As the road bends, our view extends to the entire farm, and it is beautiful! The winter wheat is growing, tractors are busy, and cows are grazing.

It was only a couple of weeks ago that the cows started grazing in this area right next to the road. Kim loves cows, and she always wanted us to get a cow. So now Kim is able to see cows every day without me having to feed them and clean up after them. God is good! Just seeing the cows ahead encourages Kim to walk faster.

Today, as I passed the cows, I gazed at the wire that the farmer used for their fence. It was only one wire and not a very thick wire at that.

Now these cows are young and strong. There are maybe twenty of them, each weighing around one thousand pounds. I turned around and looked at Kim, wondering, *Can these guys break out of that fence and hurt Kim?*

On our way home, I saw Ryan, Mr. Beer's grandson. After telling him how much Kim and I enjoy our daily walks, I asked him about the cows and if they would ever break through the wire. He assured me that, even though they are strong, they would never do that. The cows just stay where they are and enjoy the fresh spring green grass. They don't use their thousand pounds of power to break free.

Waddling back home with the dogs and Kim trailing behind me, not missing a beat of her music, I thought about those cows. Then I began to think about the power that is in me. I don't mean power like from muscles; I mean power from the Holy Spirit who lives in me. This power is more than snapping a few wires. This is a power so strong it raised Jesus from the dead! Now this is amazing power.

Jesus, please help me to remember the power you have given me in the Holy Spirit—to love you with every part of me and to love others the way I love myself.

TULLY, THE RAG DOLL

You know I have two golden retrievers, Anaiah and Tully. Kim is always asking everyone to pray for Tully, and there is a reason. He is naughty. Last night, while we were all sleeping, I heard a small crash. We are all living in the basement because of the kitchen remodeling, so no one can do anything without everyone hearing it. Well, Tully pulled down Paul's jeans, shirt, and socks—along with the lamp. Right off his high dresser! Paul had put the clothes high up to keep them out of Tully's reach because the night before Tully had grabbed his clothes off the chair. I guess that didn't work, putting the clothes high up.

Tully turns into a rag doll when I want him to move. For example, he and Anaiah love to go in the car when I go on errands. I lift up the hatchback, and Anaiah hops right in. Tully will just sit on the ground and melt into a puddle. He's afraid to jump in (he has missed a few times), and he's not big on me picking up his front paws to lay on the edge of the car. So, he slumps down. It's like I am picking up pudding with a fork!

What does this have to do with me? With Jesus?

There have been times in my life when I know Jesus wants me to do something, and I just feel like flopping down like a rag doll, like Tully. Jesus wants me to go up to someone and talk with them and welcome them, but I don't. I lay there just like Tully. Maybe Jesus wants me to say, "I'm sorry." But I refuse to do it; I lay there just like Tully. There have been times I know Jesus wants me to share his love for others and I am quiet. I'm afraid to talk to them about Jesus. I refuse to do it; I lay there just like Tully. There are times God has told me to love my neighbors, but I don't; I lay there just like Tully.

Many times I just want my own way. I just want time to myself. All by myself. But God wants me to keep on giving. He wants me to keep on loving. Jesus wants me to serve like he did and not be like Tully.

1 JOHN 5:2–5

Here is how we know that we love God's children. We know it when we love God and obey his commands. In fact, here is what it means to love God. We love him by obeying his commands. And his commands are not hard to obey. That's because everyone who is a child of God has won the battle over the world. Our faith has won the battle for us. Who is it that has won the battle over the world? Only the person who believes that Jesus is the Son of God.

ZZZZ . . .

In the mornings, when I wake up early, I get a cup of coffee. Then I pull out my Bible and make sure the dog bed is right next to me. Tully tries to beat Anaiah to the fluffy dog bed, but lately I make sure Anaiah is the one who gets to the bed first. Tully always wants what Anaiah has.

A few weeks ago, while I was reading the Bible, I looked over and saw the sweetest thing. Anaiah was fast asleep on the dog bed, happily wagging her tail. Dogs wag their tails when they are happy and content. Maybe Anaiah was having a happy dream. Maybe she was dreaming she was running on the beach. Or maybe she was dreaming she got a bone. I'll never know why her tail was wagging, but it made me wonder: *If I had a tail, would it be wagging when I slept?*

Anaiah reminds me that I can be happy, whether working or resting, knowing that God is taking care of everything.

Sometimes in the middle of the night, I'll wake up. I'm not happy and content like Anaiah. Instead, I wake up thinking about all I have to do the next day, or I wake up thinking about someone who might be having a hard time. Some nights, I'm not at all like Anaiah, happy and wagging my tail while I'm sleeping. I think I'm more like Tully. Sometimes in the middle of the night, I hear him get into the trash or pull down the towels or steal Kim's favorite stuffed animal.

Sometimes when I wake up in the middle of the night, I pray. I pray about the things I'm worried about, or I pray about the work that needs to be done the next day. But almost every time, when I wake up, I say this verse to myself:

ISAIAH 26:3

LORD, you will give perfect peace to those who commit themselves to be faithful to you. That's because they trust in you.

I'M STRESSED!

PHILIPPIANS 4:6–7a

Don't worry about anything. No matter what happens,
tell God about everything. Ask and pray, and give thanks to him.
Then God's peace will watch over your hearts and your minds.
He will do this because you belong to Christ Jesus.

I've always had a dog. Our first dog, Mickey, was huge! He took up the back seat of our Volkswagen Beetle. Then we got Riley. My daughter, Ashley, cut his fur because she wanted to be a hairdresser. Sweet Riley just sat there and let her snip away at his tail and little beard. Then came Cooper.

When we first saw Cooper with his brothers and sisters, we immediately noticed that his backyard had craters like the moon. Potholes everywhere! But we fell in love with him and happily took him home.

Kim particularly loved Cooper. She used him to pull herself up at the back door, and they looked out at our yard together, which now looked like the moon!

Oh, Cooper! Every time the back door opened, Cooper went out. Ugh! It was so frustrating. Cooper didn't run away; he sniffed away. Sniffing at anything and everything. I would go after him and look for the white tip of his tail to track and find him.

One thing Cooper didn't like was being alone. He bayed (kind of like how a dog sings), he scratched the doors, and he chewed. We didn't own a dog crate. Crates were not used forty or fifty years ago like they are today. There really wasn't a place to put Cooper to keep him safe and our stuff safe, except for the basement.

We had this room in the basement. The kind of room kids never want to go in because it is creepy. But there wasn't anything for him to wreck in the room, so we thought all was good. One day, we left him because we had to visit friends. We gave him a blanket, water bowl, and toys to keep him warm and happy. After a few hours, we came back and found that he tried to chew up the door to get out. He even chewed the frame around the door. Oh my. I called my vet and asked for suggestions. He said, "Get some Tabasco sauce and soak the door and the frame with it. Cooper will not go near it!"

So that is just what I did. I got two bottles of Tabasco sauce and almost painted the door and frame with it. It stunk to high heaven!

That night, we had to leave Cooper in the basement because we had to go to my parents' house. We left him in his special room with his blanket, water bowl, toys, and now even a bone. As I shut the door, which reeked of Tabasco, Cooper began "singing."

We got home late that night, got out of the car, and noticed all was quiet. We all walked into the dark house, and you'll never guess who greeted us: Cooper! There he was, wagging that white-tipped tail.

How in the world did he get out of that basement room? we all wondered.

I walked down the basement stairs and looked to the right—a hole. A huge hole! He ate the door. He even ate the frame around the door. "He likes Tabasco sauce!" I yelled upstairs.

Cooper got so stressed when he was left alone. I have things that stress me too. Jesus helps me remember not to worry.

WHAT TO MY WONDERING EYES SHOULD APPEAR?

We once lived in a very old house beside a creek. It had a small kitchen with a big window that looked out over the creek. I had a bird feeder hanging on a tree limb near that window. I loved to look at the birds come and go while I was working at the sink (and with six kids, I was at the sink a lot). I could also see the barnyard from this window.

In the mornings, I am the first to wake up. I make a cup of coffee and grab my Bible. One morning as I was passing by the big window to make my coffee, something caught my eye. I put on my glasses because I thought my eyes were playing tricks on me. Hmm. Then I thought I must really be tired because I wasn't seeing straight. Could that really be a bear at our bird feeder? A bear! He was leaning against the tree, batting the bird feeder with his paw, and eating the seeds as they fell! I just stood there watching as he chomped away. The more I watched, it became obvious that he was just a cub.

I wondered what I should do. Do I just assume he'll go away? Is his mom around? Could he get hurt by a car? Maybe I should call the police? Yes, I decided to call the police.

The police came and discussed what should be done. They got in touch with the state police while the bear moseyed around. The goats were watching, but the sheep (who get scared easily)

ran away. By this time, my dogs were barking, waking everybody up in the house!

Soon two men came. They had a special container on the back of their truck. The plan was to shoot a dart into the bear that would make him fall asleep. While he was asleep, they would place him in the container and drive him up to the Pocono mountains.

The man who had the dart gun shot and missed three times. Finally, the other man took the dart gun, aimed it at the bear, and hit his target. The bear started to slow down. Really slow down. Then he sat down. Then he laid down. Then he was out, sound asleep!

It took four men to pick him up and lay him into the container. I asked the man before they drove off if they could tell me how the cub was when he got to the mountains. They reported that he was asleep the entire way and only started to wake up when they stopped the truck! He was able to waddle out of the container, right into the forest.

How did the cub get to my house? The ranger said he probably wandered away from his mom and just moseyed down to our house, following the creeks.

I thought of how sometimes I mosey away from God. I just go on my own way, following something, and leave him out. Then I get into trouble too.

We—every one of us—have strayed away like this bear! We left the path God wanted us to go on and decided to roam on our own without God. But my God is such a good Father (or bear-keeper!). He knows all the places I wander and brings me back home.

ISAIAH 53:6

All of us are like sheep [or bears!]. We have wandered away from God. All of us have turned to our own way. And the LORD has placed on his servant the sins of all of us.

TO THE RESCUE!

JOHN 3:16–17

Jesus said, "God so loved the world that he gave his one and only Son. Anyone who believes in him will not die but will have eternal life. God did not send his Son into the world to judge the world. He sent his Son to save the world through him."

If you came to our house to look at the boys and goats, you would notice that they are separated by a wire fence. It hasn't always been this way, but something happened.

Now before I tell you what happened, remember that fainting goats really faint!

One day, Chezlee and Edith were in the field with Chuckie and Kisses. As usual, Chuckie and Kisses were playing, pulling each other around the field with the dog pull toy. I finished feeding and cleaning up after them, so I went into the house.

Not too long after this, I heard the boys braying. And when they bray, I can hear them loud and clear. The boys are kind of like an alarm. When they bray, something is usually wrong.

When I got outside, Chezlee was in the barn, and he was bleeding from his arm—kind of like his armpit. I called the vet, and the vet came out and laid him on the ground. He discovered that Chezlee was bleeding from a bite. One of the boys broke his skin with their big teeth! The vet had to stitch up Chezlee.

The vet knows the boys, and he knows all the goats. Neither of us could figure out what went wrong, but we agreed that this was probably a one-time thing. Just the same, I planned to keep an eye on the boys and Chezlee.

So that is what I did. From my kitchen window, I kept an eye. And what my eyes saw was something I never expected.

Kisses was playing with Chezlee. Well, what do fainting goats do when they get excited and happy? They faint. And that is what Chezlee did. He went right down! This made Kisses scared because he thought something was wrong with Chezlee. So he tried to pull him up with his teeth. Now Chezlee really "froze" because he was scared of Kisses using his teeth to get him up. This happened over and over! Kisses tried to get Chezlee up, then Chezlee would faint because he was afraid of Kisses's help.

Finally, Kisses helped Chezlee back to the small barn, but the only way he could carry Chezlee was by pulling him with his teeth!

Oh my goodness! I called the vet again, and poor Chezlee needed more stitches.

I told the vet what happened. He almost couldn't believe it. The vet explained that Kisses probably thought Chezlee couldn't get back to the small barn by himself. Animals know it isn't good to be left out in a field. They have an instinct to hide if they've been hurt, so other animals won't attack them when they are weak. Kisses thought he was rescuing Chezlee.

So now, our goats are separated from the boys. They really do love one another. But fainting goats just faint, and sweet donkeys want to help them up!

Kisses tried to rescue Chezlee, but he wasn't really the best rescuer for the job.

But I do know a wonderful Rescuer—One who is just perfect for the job. Jesus came to rescue you and me from sin, and because he did this, he also rescued us from death! You and I will live forever because of the greatest rescue ever!

CRIMPING THE FUR

Paul, Kim, Anaiah, Tully, and I have been living in our basement because of the construction going on in our house. One of the things that has been challenging in the mornings has been to "fix my face," as my mother used to say. "Fixing your face" doesn't mean to get a facelift, but rather it means to put on makeup and try to hide the large, puffy, dark bags under my eyes that I inherited from my dad. It also means to put a little color on my lips.

Anyway, living in the basement, my face is not fixed most mornings, and I am lucky if I can find my comb for my hair!

Some mornings I've even called hair "fur." One day I said to Kim, "Let's comb our 'fur' before we go to work." Another day, I came in from cleaning up the barnyard and exclaimed, "My 'fur' is blowing all over outside today!"

But there is someone in our house who really does look like he combs his fur. Actually, it looks like he crimps his fur. It is Tully. If you look at the top of Tully's ears, it looks like they have been crimped. They are all wavy! I have had people ask me, "Do you crimp his fur?" In between my giggles, I reply, "Look at my hair! It hardly looks like I comb it. Do you really think I crimp Tully's fur?" And then we both laugh!

Did you know in the Bible Jesus gives us his definition of beauty? He tells us about true beauty. He says it comes from the inside.

I need to tell you, Tully is beautiful on the outside with his crimped fur, and he also has a sweetness about him. He always wants to run to the door when someone comes in and bring them a gift, like his favorite blanket or toy. I'm not too sure about him having a quiet spirit though!

But I'm not certain about a quiet spirit in me either! Some days, it is hard to have a quiet spirit, to have peace. I need to remember that God calls me his child. My name is written on his hands, and everything is under his control—and it will all work out for good.

1 PETER 3:3–4

Fancy hairstyles don't make you beautiful. Wearing gold jewelry or fine clothes doesn't make you beautiful. Instead, your beauty comes from inside you. It is the beauty of a gentle and quiet spirit. Beauty like this doesn't fade away. God places great value on it.

CHRISTMAS STORY: TULLIFIED

Paul, Kim, and I went to a special Christmas tree farm this year. After driving to the farm, it didn't take us long to find the perfect tree. The branches were full and fluffy all the way around. It was the prettiest and tallest tree our family ever got!

We had the perfect spot for our tree to stand—right next to our kitchen that looks out onto Mr. Beer's farm. Our neighbors would be able to see the little lights twinkling from the road!

I ran to the attic to get my tree decorations. We have many beautiful ornaments, the kind of ornaments that I wrap up individually with tissue paper so each one of them is safe from breaking while stored away. Some of the ornaments go back to my grandparents. One of them is a soldier that goes back to the Civil War. Many are glass ornaments that my aunts gave us every year as the kids were growing up. Santas of all shapes, sizes, and colors. Snowmen that glitter from sequins. So many angels it makes you think you are part of the heavenly host that welcomed baby Jesus! Ornaments that all our kids, all six of them, made throughout their elementary school years. And then the tree topper. Two paper angels that Kim made when she was four years old. And the crooked smiles on these angels that almost shout out, "Glory to God in the highest!"

As time went on, packages were opened under the tree, and meals were enjoyed around it. One day, I had just taken Tully and Anaiah for a walk. I took off Anaiah's leash, but I forgot to take off Tully's. Well, I don't think I told you yet, but Tully also loves the Christmas tree. He likes to get a drink out of the tree stand. And after a walk, Tully gets thirsty. So Tully got the drink. Then he walked around the tree, gazing at the ornaments on the lower branches.

Continuing his pacing around the tree, he noticed all the felt-stuffed reindeer. Tully continued his circling. Snowmen, Santas, delicate paper ornaments—so much to smell! Then it happened. Tully walked away from the tree, and the tree followed him. Tully ran away from the tree, and the tree ran after him. Oh no, the tree was "Tullified"!

Unaware of the leash wrapping around the tree as he paced, Tully just froze in the middle of the crash. Glass everywhere, but he didn't get hurt. After cleaning up, I assured Tully that we

loved him and we all do things that get messed up. Tully has a loving heart, but he's not always aware of his environment!

Oh Tully, so much confusion. So much noise. So much clean-up. It reminds me of Christmas night. How Mary and Joseph wondered why there wasn't any room for Mary to have a baby. No room except for a small barn. The roaring sound of heaven shouting out that the Savior of the world was born! There was so much to cleanup that it took the Savior going to the cross to die for our sins. What a night. Rejoice! Hallelujah! Christ has come!

LUKE 2:10–11

But the angel said to them, "Do not be afraid. I bring you good news. It will bring great joy for all the people. Today in the town of David a Savior has been born to you. He is the Messiah, the Lord."

ACKNOWLEDGMENTS

Thank you Barb Juliani for inviting me to 415 to eat some of your mom's homemade cookies, cry with your dad who invited me to ask Jesus into my life, and meet your brother Paul who narrowly escaped the math book I threw out of your bedroom window. Also, I'm so grateful you enjoyed these stories enough to encourage New Growth to publish them.

Thank you Dan Stelzer for your warmth and encouragement during this project. Thank you Brad Woodard for making the animals come to life with your art!

Thank you Michele Walton and Sherri Hughes for jumping in with your help and skill in the many areas I needed help and skill!

Thank you Mr. Beer for letting me run every day on your gravel road that bends onto a view of your beautiful farm. Every day, through all the seasons, it is breathtaking!

Thank you Jesus for Paul who understands my love of animals even as we go through our annual budget for the last fifty years!

Thank you Jesus for my kids: Courtney, Ashley, John, Kim, Andrew, and Emily. I remember Ashley calling me on the phone, shortly before she went to heaven, telling me how blessed I am to have grandkids. My cup overflows. How amazing you are, Abba. To you ALL glory. All.

Holy, holy, holy!
Lord God almighty!
All Thy works shall praise Thy name
  in earth and sky and sea.
Holy, holy, holy!
Merciful and mighty!
You are God in three persons, blessed Trinity!

(Reginald Heber, "Holy, Holy, Holy")